POETRY C

GREAT MINDS

Your World...Your Future...YOUR WORDS

From East & West Sussex
Edited by Jessica Woodbridge

Young**Writers**

First published in Great Britain in 2005 by:
Young Writers
Remus House
Coltsfoot Drive
Peterborough
PE2 9JX
Telephone: 01733 890066
Website: www.youngwriters.co.uk

SB ISBN 1 84460 874 3

Foreword

This year, the Young Writers' 'Great Minds' competition proudly presents a showcase of the best poetic talent selected from over 40,000 up-and-coming writers nationwide.

Young Writers was established in 1991 to promote the reading and writing of poetry within schools and to the youth of today. Our books nurture and inspire confidence in the ability of young writers and provide a snapshot of poems written in schools and at home by budding poets of the future.

The thought, effort, imagination and hard work put into each poem impressed us all and the task of selecting poems was a difficult but nevertheless enjoyable experience.

We hope you are as pleased as we are with the final selection and that you and your family continue to be entertained with *Great Minds From East & West Sussex* for many years to come.

Contents

Shanice Hersey (12)	41
Lewis Williams (12)	42
Jessica Browne (12)	42
J'aime Luvin (12)	43
Jade Ward (12)	43
Tyler Anderson (12)	44
Kyle Tansley (13)	44
Violet Jarman (14)	45
Constance Crowhurst (12)	45
Jessica Harms (12)	46
Nicole Evans (13)	46
Kimberley Jones (14)	47
Rebecca Cumbers (13)	47
William Ford (12)	48
Lewis Breach (12)	48
Louise Bliss (12)	49
Hollie Stacey (12)	49
Michael Roberts (12)	50
Roxanne Davey (12)	50
Eddie Edge (12)	51
Jasmine Hunn (12)	51
Leanne Ford (12)	52
Conor Phillips (12)	52
Eloisa Mae Gordon (12)	53
Alexandra Craven (12)	54
Kelly Wheller (12)	54
Amber Henley (12)	55
Toby Bassett (12)	56
Sam Walsh (12)	57
Abby Winter (12)	58
Katie Davey (12)	58
Danielle Louise Fisher (11)	59
Sophie Waters (12)	59
Nicola Barton (14)	60
Aron Jacob (12)	60
Jamie Finch (15)	61
Sarah Greenan (12)	61
Danielle Didcock (15)	62
Sohpie Dowdeswell (17)	62
Kerrie Bailey (15)	63
Jamie Saunders (13)	64
Daniel Gray (13)	64

Natasha Barwise (12)	65
Adam Nelson (13)	65
Charlie Jones (12)	66
Jack Peevor (13)	67
Usman Sarwar (15)	68
Rebecca Cooper (11)	68
Jason Raj (14)	69
Maria Rowsell (12)	70
Danielle Louise Pay (12)	70
Claire Hewitt (13)	71

Lavant House School

Maisie McGuirk (11)	71
Hannah Martin (11)	72
Chloë Keir Watson (11)	72
Florence Christie (11)	73
Rebecca Richards (12)	74
Suzanne Peckham (12)	74
Harriet Mullins (16)	75
Louise Cavanagh (14)	75
Natalie Anscombe (14)	76
Ayesha Miles (14)	76
Molly Richard (14)	77
Chloe Oecken (14)	77
Harriet Elsom (14)	78
Charlotte Torr (14)	78
Marcia Miles (12)	79
Holly Edwards (11)	79
Georgiana Upfold (12)	80
Connie Chen (12)	80
Francesca Betes (12)	81
Amelia Hendy (12)	81
Alexandra Gibson (13)	82
Daisy Christie (14)	82
Alex Day (12)	83
Samantha Day (14)	83
Jemma Simpson (11)	84
Georgia Ellis (12)	84

Longhill High School

Chelsea Edmeads (14)	85
Emma Shahmir (12)	85
Emily Adsett (14)	86
Bethany Mitten (12)	86
Brigit Belden (13)	87
Katie Stevens (12)	87
Elouise Date (14)	88
Annabelle Lee (12)	88
Vicky Clarkson (12)	89
James Foot (12)	89
Tyler Goatcher (11)	90
Ruby Mitchell (12)	90
James Yates (11)	91
Cara Richardson (14)	92
Thomas Simpson (11)	92
Victor Laidler (14)	93
Zeshaan Zaidi (13)	94
Danielle Hilton (15)	94
Karl Stepney (13)	95
Lucy Davies (14)	95
Emma Gillam (15)	96
Grace Baddiley (14)	96
Courtney Darby (14)	97
Arla Kayne (14)	97
Ben Taylor (14)	98
Tonie Lam (13)	99
Alice Cloud (13)	100
Lily Robertson (13)	100
Joanna Osborne (12)	101
Shelley Hunt (12)	101
Michael Overlaet (13)	102
Nick Taylor (14)	103
James Hart (12)	104
Jordan Green (11)	104
James Scott (11)	105
Charlotte Bishop-Williams (12)	105
Rosie Parsons (13)	106
Paige Burt (11)	106
Andrew Baker (13)	107
Sophie Butterstone (11)	107

Millais School

Northease Manor School

Anna Maycock-Frame (14)   179
Shannon Elliston (11)   180
Jack Roberts (11)   180
Ellen Redhouse (11)   180
Rebecca Bentley (15)   181
Lucas Rajpaul (15)   182

Patcham House Special School
Sophie Blume (12)   182
Kelly Gunn (11)   182
Keifer Hall (11)   183
David Hall (11)   183
Christopher Hammond (13)   183
Evan Hilton (11)   184
Jamie Moore (11)   184
Lawrence Harmer-Strange (11)   184
Bruce Leathead (13)   185
Sarah Steele (12)   185
Joseph Cooke (11)   186
Leanne Dearling (11)   186

Rydon Community College
Charlotte Bothamley (11)   187
William Steer (11)   187
Michael Harkness (11)   188
Julia Hartley (11)   188
Will Chambers (11)   189
Georgia Pettman (11)   190
Chanteé Jansen Van Rensburg (12)   190
Chelsea Snoad (11)   191
Joe Fish (12)   191
Natalie Bate (11)   192
Dan Brennan (11)   192
Joshua Rideout (11)   193
William Busby (11)   193
Megan Harber (11)   194
Lewis Yearsley (11)   194
David McKilligin (11)   195
Becky Howie (11)   195
Imogen Bowen-Davies (11)   196
Taome Gardner (12)   197

The Poems

Through My Eyes

I saw the sky
I saw the sea
Both beneath me
Both within me

My blood is like the sea
For its journey never ends
My breath is like the sky
For it is always changing

When I look at the sea
I see my sorrow washed away
When I look at the sky
I feel my sadness blown away.

Steven Elderton (14)

Underground

I was bored one day, so I grabbed my coat
And I went down to the underground,
Saw the people in their metal coffins,
All of a sudden, fire and sound,
I saw the faces of the screaming, they were mine,
Saw the faces of the clean-up crew,
Saw no faces of the dead, but they were mine,
Saw not faces, but saw right through.

So I took a trip down to the morgue,
Saw the cold, white ,dead, embalmed,
Saw a family, eyes glistening in the sun,
Laying a single rose on her palm,
I saw the face of the mother, it was mine,
Saw the face of the sister, it was mine,
Saw the face of the father, it was mine,
Saw the face of the dead, it was mine.

I was bored one day, so I grabbed my coat
And I went down to the underground,
Saw the people in their metal coffins,
All of a sudden, fire and sound,
As I called for help, I saw a man,
An evil glint in his eyes,
Opened up his jacket, saw a coil of wire
And he pulled the cord, we both died.

So I took a trip down to the morgue,
I was the dead, embalmed,
I saw the family, weeping in the rain,
Laid a single rose on my palm.

Robert Gordon (16)
Haywards Heath College

Life

If I were there,
Watching sand grains hijack the wind,
Like a sea of jewels in the air.

The waves, once tranquil,
Stumble drunkenly on the shore,
Leaving with them a foam, cloud-white;
The sound strict and hollow,
Lives and dies,
Lives and dies.

And now, an autumn avenue of trees,
Their leaves a bitter red,
Bound together by fate.

With every turn,
One more falls.
No time to mourn the loss,
For those lying limp on the crowded floor,
What red are now but grey,
Had lived but now are dead,
Had lived but now are dead.

And now I am sitting
Once more at an empty desk,
For once was seen, is now written;
Once was lived, is now left;
And the soul behind the sitting,
Has life but now is dead,
Has life but now is dead.

Ashley Mogford (17)
Haywards Heath College

Chocolate

Craving, hunger,
Open lips,
Dribble oozing in my mouth,
As I reach out with my trembling fingertips,
Tearing the crackling paper,
Crunching in my palm,
Dark and creamy it appears,
The chocolate's delicious charm.
Rich cocoa smells waft in my nose,
Closer and closer the chocolate goes,
My body is in a dreamy trance,
Sweet and smooth,
It touches my tongue.
A scrumptious taste,
A blissful moment,
Munching, melting,
Sticky, gooey,
While I lick my lips and fingers.
Depression engulfs me,
As my chocolate heaven ends,
But my greedy belly cries
And I grab another bar.

Claire Stokes (15)
Hazelwick School

Sherbet

S herbet is the greatest sweet
H issing and bubbling when you eat
E xtremely fizzy on my tongue
R eminds me of the feeling when being stung
B lueberry, orange, all flavours are great
E xploding reaction, makes my mouth inflate
T he aftertaste of sherbet makes me feel jolly!

Kenny Young (12)
Hazelwick School

Cracked Up

I wake up in the morning, rise and shine,
Making money through the life of crime,
I'm reminiscing what a night,
Every day having one-way fights,
Thinking if my actions were worth that chain,
Thinking if my actions were that humane,
Escape this world by smoking trees,
Mug people 24-7 and then count my Gs,
Everybody be giving me beef, let's keep it brief,
I'm a thief and money is all I seek,
Yes, I got dreams, but this is my life,
Not a good one when you got no home, no wife,
Nobody loves me, so I don't believe in sympathy,
To be honest, I don't care what anyone thinks of me,
It don't matter who they are, I just got one view,
I get up, go out and jack anyone I choose,
I'm up for anything, as long as I get my dough,
I don't care if I kill, so watch where you go,
Pick-pocket to get money from people's wallets,
Take advantage and get money from drunken alcoholics,
At the age of five I lost my folks,
At the age of eight I started to smoke,
I'm not an angel, I'm not the pope,
Make dirty money by selling dope,
People live life based on hope,
People live life like it's some joke,
Not funny when you're addicted to weed, speed and coke,
I tried to change what I became, but it's a shame,
Because I still remain in this dirty game,
I had a cold start, I could have been so smart,
But it didn't go my way, so I've got a cold heart,
I've been struggling from the beginning,
That's why I've been hustling for a living,
Tried to change my rep, but this world is not forgiving,
It's hard when you got no love, no help,
But in this dog-eat-dog world, you've got to survive by yourself.

Bhavesh Nayee (14)
Hazelwick School

She Goes To Him

She lies there, waiting
Her eyes close and slowly open again
Each breath an effort

She feels sleepy
And closes her eyes, slowly
Reluctantly

When she heard it
A sound
The sound

The sound of birds and beasts
The sound of love, of hate
The sound of pain, of joy

The sound of life

The sound of death

She opens her eyes
And there he is

Waiting

Watching

Ready for her

She feels nothing

No pain

Nothing

Just regret

Regret at not having lived
When she had the chance

She closes her eyes for the last time

And goes to him.

Charlotte Louise O'Rourke (13)
Hazelwick School

School Life

I walk the empty corridors
Thinking what used to be
A school, so lively
What I could not see

I walk the empty corridors
Alone and no company
Tables on their tops
No chairs, not any

I walk the empty corridors
Through the dust and grime
Children up to mischief
Children up to crime

I walk the empty corridors
The smell of disallowed smoke
Secret drink and gum
Enough to make me choke

I walk the empty corridors
Where couples were pried together
Young love, haunts me
Sadness, no, not ever

I walk the empty corridors
Homework late, detentions come
Diaries out, pen in hand
Oh, what fun . . .

I walked the empty corridors
To be done never again
My time has been and gone
School is over.

Karen-Marie Davis (14)
Hazelwick School

The Night Sky

Here in the dark do I endlessly lie,
Gazing at the stars in the clear night sky.

My troubles, my pain and my thoughts are lost,
As so are my fellows which I don't wish to lose at any cost.

From no-man's-land do I hear endless cries,
But what can I say, no one dare tries;

To help those that are injured in no-man's-land,
For that is the area we are all banned.

Our life is sheer hell,
Everyone can tell.

To all those young, brave heroes who lost their lives,
I hear the cry of their saddened wives.

The stench is rotten,
The place is forgotten;

Where my old mates lie,
Dead amongst the night sky.

Though I see how hard they fought
And remember clearly the songs they taught.

My eyes look above at the heroes in the sky,
They rest in peace as they watch the days go by.

Saliah Malik (15)
Hazelwick School

Poptarts!

P opping in
O r
P opping out
T oaster goodies
A re
R eally
T asty
S urprises!

Lauren Glanville & David Ainsworth (14)
Hazelwick School

Chocolate

I am a chocoholic and I'm proud to admit it,
I much prefer my chocolate to the average old biscuit,
Chocolate comes in all different shapes and sizes,
I jump for joy when I receive them for surprises.

I get given chocolate quite regularly,
Every Valentine's Day in February,
Santa brings me chocolate coins,
It helps me grow my bones and joints,
The Easter bunny brings a bunch,
Of chocolate eggs I like to munch.

Eight tasty chocolate bars a day,
Keeps my foul mood away,
Chocolate milk, dark brown and white,
Gives my mouth pleasure and delight,
Chocolate feels nice when it melts on my tongue,
I need it to live, like I need my lung.

I can't get enough of that wonderful stuff,
No matter how much I have, it just ain't enough,
I am an addict, yes it's true,
I'm a chocoholic, are you too?

Anneka Redley (14)
Hazelwick School

Fire!

Fire! Fire!
We hear the call,
Somebody's dying,
Help us all!

The Fire Brigade come,
But their work has been done,
By a strange someone,
Oh my Lord! It's my mum!

Richard Cooling (14)
Hazelwick School

Poems

Poems can be short,
Poems can be long,
Poems can be sad,
Poems can be fun,
Poems can be interesting,
Poems can be boring,
Poems can be rhyming,
Poems can be not,
Poems can be strange,
Poems can be weird,
Poems can be the same,
Poems can be different,
Poems can be whispered,
Poems can be sung,
But the best poems of all
Are the ones that get *written!*

Alice Chalker (14)
Hazelwick School

Strawberries And Cream

Mouth-watering, red, juicy strawberries,
Coated in thick, whipped cream,
That's the dessert of my dream!

Sausages and fluffy, Yorkshire pudding,
Covered in smooth, runny gravy,
That's something I've loved since I was a baby!

Crispy bacon, mushrooms and egg,
Swarming in tons of tomato sauce,
I'll eat that anytime, it's my favourite course!

I'll eat most foods,
Potatoes, sandwiches, pasta bake,
But sprouts are something I'll never touch!

Vicki Pritchard Murphy (13)
Hazelwick School

Doner Meat!

Doner meat
You make me so sweet
You're good with chips
Also nice with dips
With ketchup and burger sauce
You sometimes make my main course
You come in a sheet of paper
Some people say they hate ya
I get you at the Kebab shop
You always come on top
Of the chips, cos you're the best part
Oh doner meat you're always in my heart
You only cost two pounds
I love you to the ground
You're made out of lamb
You make me open a can
You're so yummy
I need you in my tummy
I want you, oh doner meat
In my mind, you'll never be beat!

Adam Marshall (14)
Hazelwick School

Snowflake

I caught a snowflake in my hand
and whispered softly, 'Do all that you can
if you leave me now, I have nothing left
so don't scare me like this, half to death.'
I opened my hand slowly, but wished
what if that was our last ever kiss?
Am I prepared to say goodbye
or am I going to break down and cry?
When I opened my hand, the snowflake had gone
and I can't bring you back, but with me you belong.

Emma Constant (15)
Hazelwick School

Food, Food, All Around The World

Italian food is the best,
Like pizza, pasta and the rest,
We love their sauce,
With every other course.

Food, food, all around the world.

When spicy foods and dips are here,
You know the Mexicans must be near,
With tacos, fajitas and salsa galore,
These are the foods we all adore.

Food, food, all around the world.

Americans love the fattest food,
A meal to match every mood,
Burgers, hot dogs, they just rule,
These are the foods that make us drool.

Richard Cooling & Stuart Morris (14)
Hazelwick School

Habits

We're all cosy in our beds, snug as a bug
That's great

We have shelter, food and comfort
That's wonderful

We're big and strong, we can fight our own battles
More than we could ever wish for

Big, fat bulldozers killing the small, what do they have?
Nothing at all
That's horrible.

Bernice Broom
Hazelwick School

Animal Movement

Mice scurry as they hurry,
Rabbits twitch when they itch,
Lions creep, then retreat,
Birds fly into the sky,
Tigers stroll before they roll,
Badgers scramble as they amble,
Foxes quake and shake,
Horses banter as they canter,
Squirrels zoom into their doom,
Cows sway when they eat hay,
Cheetahs prefer to run for fun,
There's always a trace of a snail race.

Laura Haselum (14)
Hazelwick School

Death!

It lies in mystery
a place in everyone's head
for some it's feared
but who knows what it's like to be dead!

Some think you go to Heaven
some think you go to Hell
some think you're just gone forever
but who knows, no one can tell.

When it comes, you can't tell anyone about it
or what it feels and does to you
everyone wonders about the possibilities
but who knows? I want to know too.

Amy Barden (14)
Hazelwick School

The Ballad Of The Earthquake

It was a hot day
And children were doing PE and becoming dirty
in the playground muck
On this spring May
Children were playing, when it struck.

There were shakes and rocks
And there were cracks in the wall
Children were screaming
As, into the lava fell soft foam balls.

Children were screaming
Teachers were frightened
Parents did not know
Until the phone call came in and they froze,
stiff and tightened.

The rescuers were there
Hoping there would be life
And then they realised that
The school had gone, even the last cafeteria knife.

A lesson has been learnt
That one day, scientists can detect
So one day they can alert a school somewhere
And they can protect!

Johnathan Harrold (12)
Ifield Community College

My Mum Says

My mum says to eat your greens
I think she is being mean.
My mum says eat your veg
So I chuck it off the window ledge.
My mum says peas are good
I would ban them if I could.
Broccoli stinks, cabbage is worse
I think vegetables are a curse.

Zara Akhtar (11)
Ifield Community College

Ocean's Wilderness

The ocean glistens in the light,
Which shines ever so bright,
Feasting away at the land,
Coughing out the shimmering sand.

Swallowing the sand and stones,
Like a dog chewing a juicy bone,
Ships and boats they sink,
Rotting away as soon as the sea winks.

As dolphins glide, side to side,
Imagine living in a sea, ever so wide!
Having an entertaining day,
All day the sea creatures perform a play!

The ferocious ocean rages in the storm!
The sea stops at dawn.
The animals are safe and sound,
The ocean is like a giant playground!

The sea is azure,
The sea is turquoise,
The sea is like a gleaming rainbow!
The sea is moving to and fro.

Under the sea is treasure full of wonder!
Creating ways to shine,
There's an ocean out there,
It twinkles and protects,
The people wonder at the dazzling beach.

From the beginning to the end,
The sea is there!
Whistling and singing,
But sometimes it is full of rage and fear!
So beware!

Sophie Cooper (12)
Ifield Community College

The Ballad Of An Earthquake Disaster

It happened in October days
An earthquake took place
Early in the evening
The horror on people's faces.

It had happened in New York
Lots had still survived
But seventy-six died
Even children and wives.

They had all been warned
They all regretted it
No notice was taken
Not listening one bit.

Now what do they do
Without their loved ones?
Thinking they were here
But nothing can be done.

Laying in the dark
Under the dust
They lie until they are found
Rotting like the rust.

Listen when something is happening
Listen, you must
Don't ignore the truth
Or you'll end up like us.

Zahira Gulam (13)
Ifield Community College

The Sword

S lashing, fearsome, silver sword
W hooshing through the air
O gres and dragons beware
R un now, it's not too late
D on't face me or you will meet your fate!

Carl Whittick (12)
Ifield Community College

Beasts Of The Mind

There lived a unicorn,
As white as snow,
Her beautiful mane,
Waved to and fro.

She also had a pointy horn,
Beautiful and smooth,
Whenever you looked at her head,
You could see a milky-white tooth.

There also lived a griffin,
With huge, powerful wings,
This creature liked jewellery
And lots of other things.

This beast looked like an eagle,
He was also like a lion,
His beak was sharp and stout
And his claws felt like iron.

The dragon lived just round the bend,
A friendly one, mind you!
His forest was vast and dense
And he never caught the flu!

His skin was as red as fire,
His teeth were sharp knives,
But he eats only cows and sheep
And when he feasts, he jives!

Pegasus wasn't as beautiful,
As strong or as huge as the others,
But she is liked, all the same,
Even the goblin seems better than her,
But Pegasus still has fame!

Joshua Humphreys (12)
Ifield Community College

The City At Night

The city at night
Was a big fright.
I wandered everywhere
Without a care.

I got into a muddle
I walked into a puddle.
I could not get dry
So I started to cry.

I tried to find my way home
But all I could see, was a phone.
There was nowhere to go
Time was passing, slow.

I wanted to go to sleep
And not hear one more peep.
Then I saw some light
There my mum was in sight.

I found my home at last
My bedtime had passed.

Westley Bailey (12)
Ifield Community College

Oh No, Not Fish!

Gross, sour, smelly fish,
I wouldn't have them on my dish,
I was told that I'd get a cold,
Actually, my weight has been lowered,
The smell just smells like a rotten well,
It suddenly didn't go down too well,
I choked and croaked and groaned,
I felt I wasn't awake,
I thought I was going to faint,
I prayed just like a saint,
I felt all right just at that minute,
Oh, how I hate the sight!

Nicole Le Feuvre (11)
Ifield Community College

The Ballad Of Nanny Morean

Nanny Morean was in the kitchen preparing her meal,
When she thought she could feel
Water on the floor,
So she opened the door.

As the water poured in,
She said with a grin,
'There must have been a leak,
That happened last week!'

When I was in Spain,
The ice froze the main
And now there's trauma,
Because it's warmer.

Now it is the summer,
Let's call a plumber,
To replace the tank,
So we have to get to the bank.

Now it's time for the clear-up to begin,
Drying the floor
And even the bin.

She should have checked,
So it didn't have an effect,
She burst the pipe,
So she best get on her bike.

Emily Burchell (12)
Ifield Community College

A Knife

A jellyfish sting,
A razor-sharp cut,
A deep scar left behind,
A sting that lasts for a while,
Makes you cry,
The pain is very strong.

Amy Reynolds (12)
Ifield Community College

The Earthquake

There was a terrible earthquake
It happened around a few towns.
Lots of houses were surrounded
With rats, mice and sounds.

Shops were destroyed
And 1500 people died.
The rest of the people
Were lucky to survive.

The earthquake separated people
Families and friends.
When the earthquake ends
They will spend their money again.

Towns began to shake
Roads began to crack.
In the news they say
'Get out of the way!'

All towns are messy
The people are in tears.
And half the people who are here
Can't bear their fear.

Rumcy Supramaniyam (12)
Ifield Community College

Pizza

Tasty toppings, greasy cheese,
More, more, more, more, more, more, please.

Tasty cheese, stuffed in crust,
That order is a definite must.

Lots of meaty options and veggie options too,
But my favourite topping of them all, will make you need the loo!

Ben Logan (11)
Ifield Community College

The Ballad Of Lilly White

When Lilly White went to the park,
With her brother, Mark,
They went on the bark.

It was night before they got home
And the street lights shone,
They knew they should phone,
Where had the time gone?

The house was all black,
None of the lights were on,
The key should have been on the rack,
Then they saw it had gone.

Mum had gone,
Where? They didn't know,
'Where should we go?'
They cried, 'No, no, no!'

The moral of this story,
Is very bright and clear,
Don't forget the time and cause worry,
To those who hold you dear.

Siobhan Coston (12)
Ifield Community College

Life

A train journey
A beginning, an end
A path that must be walked
A game that cannot be won
A gift
A curse

A box of chocolates
A three course meal
A precious jewel.
Metaphors of life.

James Grubb (13)
Ifield Community College

The Ballad Of Iraq

Turn back the pages of blasts
Which made nothing in Iraq to last
Three quarters of a city has gone and flown
What more to be left alone.

It happened during last month
The exact date was the tenth
In the middle city of an Iraq nation
After they ignored the caution.

As usual, a night before the explosion
They said, 'It might happen in television'
None of them ever cared
Or perhaps they never heard.

The reason for this revolution
Is the cruel terrorists' evolution
Now the country is without peace
Because of their assaults that never cease.

Every caution you ignore
Will give you danger, more and more.

Nuskey Mohammed Nazeerudeen (12)
Ifield Community College

Food

Chips, beans, burgers too
all having a war in the loo
and with you
with mushrooms here
and cheese there
loading their guns
with a nice, juicy pear
with chips shooting beans
and mushrooms shooting cheese
I don't like eating these.

Scott Smith (11)
Ifield Community College

The Ballad Of: Smoking Can Kill

Leonard started smoking,
Now he's choking,
He has cancer,
So he can't be a bouncer.

He is depressed,
Because he hasn't made a success,
He has gone into hospital,
Now he's lost it all.

Now he's nearly dead,
He is waiting to go, on his death bed,
He is waiting for company,
But no one is coming for him.

Now he has passed away,
He has gone away,
Now, this is no joke,
Do not smoke.

Don't get bullied into smoking, this is the moral.

Alice Arnold (12)
Ifield Community College

A Tiger

A blending machine,
Some twinkling stars,
Zebra's skin,
Pointy daggers,
An orange fuzz.

A ball of fluff,
A curled up whip,
A steady rock,
The speed of a bike,
Roar of an engine.

Daniel Austin (13)
Ifield Community College

A Destroyed Wish

I see a shadow through a door,
Makes me shiver and feels cold,
Their every footstep polishes the floor,
But something about this is as good as gold.
I try and try to figure it out,
But the shadow starts to draw near,
My shock doesn't let me move about,
Because I find that they're a large part of my fear.
A hand reaches out to hold me,
This room is no longer part of the night,
Now I can definitely see,
Then I awake, my heart full of delight,
I long to be with this shadow,
More than to be in this world and I'd rather,
Be with *him* because I feel so low
Oh, how I miss my father.

Tayiba Rahouffe (13)
Ifield Community College

A Toddler's Snack

Ice cream, ice cream all around
Chocolate squares on the ground
Flavoured sprinkles on their toes
How did they get there?
Who knows, who knows?

Apple juice in their hand
They drop it in a pile of sand
To the truck is where we go
Because they want something as cold as snow.

As the ice cream truck pulls away
That is the end of today
As we walk to the car
All I hear is blah, blah, blah!

Jodie Grinham (11)
Ifield Community College

A Nonsense Poem

A cup of cake
A piece of water
A bar of mud
A sweet shop of books
A book shop of sweets
A bath of chocolate
A zoo of children
A school of animals
A garden of books
A library of flowers
A flat with two floors
A spotty zebra
A stripy leopard
A poet writing a story
A writer writing a poem
A fish on land
A school of adults
A college of children
A sea of sand
A beach of water
An adult puppy
An adult kitten
A flying dog
A walking fish
A camel in water.

Emma Drury (11)
Ifield Community College

Potatoes

Potatoes, potatoes, in the ground,
Big ones, small ones, muddy and round.
Roasted, chipped, baked or steamed,
Boiled, croquet, sautéd or creamed.
Potatoes, potatoes, are highly nutritious,
However you cook them, they're always delicious.

Josh Rodwell (11)
Ifield Community College

Is That Fair?

Cows cooped up in a farm barn,
Unable to move,
Never walked on fresh grass,
Is that fair?

Chickens made so fat,
They can't walk,
Never smelt fresh air,
Is that fair?

Pigs killed in their thousands,
Grown for killing,
No real life,
Is that fair?

Would you like to be kept so close to someone,
That you could feel their breath in your face?
It's not fair,
Is it?

Sam Harris (12)
Ifield Community College

The Yeti Cubs

The hunters are coming
And the yeti mother flees
The hunters come up the snow-capped mountain
Filled with anger and hate
And the yeti cubs are left to their fate
Some men wanted fame and fortune
But one man wanted to help
Some people thought he was mad
Bringing the cubs to his lab
But in the end he was sad
The hunter's wives told of his madness
They knocked down his doors
And young yeti blood flooded the floors.
One yeti cub survived.

Liam Cooper (12)
Ifield Community College

Pizza

Pretty pizza delicious and sweet
It will make a lovely treat
Oozing with cheese and tasty tomatoes
That's what I like to eat

Purple pizza smelly and gross
It will make you into a ghost
Pouring out mould, that's terrible
It will make you sick for an hour!

Fabulous pizza, scrumptious and juicy
It will make you go all loopy
Mouth-watering juices flying everywhere
It's sweet, delicious over there

Disgusting pizza, revolting and grotesque
It will make you protest
Sickly juice in my throat
It will make me into a goat!

Rebecca Hawes (11)
Ifield Community College

The Weather Poem

The weather now is getting so bitter,
We are all just sitting here with a bit of a shiver.

The sun comes out and we rush outside,
But as soon as we do it goes in and hides.

The sun's gone in, the sky's getting blacker,
Then all of a sudden, we hear such a clatter,
The thunder starts, the lightning strikes,
The rain comes down with such force and might.

We rush inside to keep out of the rain
And watch the rain through the windowpane.

Mark James Hackwell (12)
Ifield Community College

The Nonsense Poem

Apples are blue
Bananas are red
People are green
Chickens are bread.

Oranges are purple
Lemons are white
Strawberries are brown
Cars are bright.

Dogs are gold,
Cats are old,
Donkeys are amber.

Houses are black
And that's a fact.

Grapes are orange
Melons are grey
People are having fun all day.

Pears are lilac
Plums are blue
Horses are yellow
I am too.

Jamie Davis (11)
Ifield Community College

The Doughnut Poem

The doughnut just lies there in the air,
just waiting to be bought with the money that is fair.
The sugar is so sweet,
it does not taste like feet.
I imagine the dough just like snow,
put it all together and the doughnut will taste better.
When you put it in your mouth
you won't be able to get it out!

Adam Dallamore (11)
Ifield Community College

The First Dragon

The first dragon emerges from his egg,
Out comes its diminutive leg,
Released from the shell,
He's a living hell.

As he continue to grow,
So does his strength,
He leaves his grotto
And swoops into the morning light.

As brave as a knight,
He observes his kingdom,
As he stretches his wings
And his talons appear.

The dragon's scales are glazed over with lava red,
He stands as high as a skyscraper,
And thicker than a brick wall,
So he cannot be budged.

As the years go by,
The dragon gets older,
His last bit of fire fades
And the light of the flame goes out.

Ashlee Jayne Smallwood (11)
Ifield Community College

Fruit Pie

Plums, pears and pineapples,
Apples, avocados and apricots,
Limes, lemons and lychees,
Covered with hot pastry,
Oh, how it was so tasty!

My pie is a fruit delight,
Don't be shy, take a bite!

Hauzlah Abowath (12)
Ifield Community College

The White Room

The white room was gleaming a very bright white,
When being by the morning sunlight.
The white wardrobe in the corner of the room,
Sitting in the shade's gloom.
The white mirror hanging on the wall,
The opposite side to the hall.
The white door on the same wall,
Leading directly to the hall.
And underneath a bright red glow,
The outside carpet colour being shown.
The white bed in the middle of it all,
With its backside facing the hall.
The white bin next to the white table,
So you are easily able,
To throw your rubbish in
And did I tell you about the white tin?
The table it lay on,
To store pens and crayons.
The white window on the wall,
Giving light to all.
In the sunlight flows
And that's how this poem goes.

Sean Wragg (11)
Ifield Community College

My Nan's Stew

Oh no! Nan's for tea
Please, no Mum, please
My nan's stew tastes like doggy poo.

She mixes it with her feet for a treat
By the time it's on the plate
She's too late, I'm gone, gone, gone!

Zoe Killick (11)
Ifield Community College

Never Give Up

The sun's blaze shines on his blond hair,
It looks so silky and fair,
As he is playing football,
Supporting his town and team,
He kicks and does throw-ins,
As I give a jolly scream,
'Well done, Lewis,' I say to him at the end,
'Good goal, good set up, well played!'
While all his friends say to him, 'Well laid!'
He bounces off, all excited,
Like a dragon that has caught his prey,
He won't forget all the compliments he was given today.

Three, two, one, *bleep* the whistle goes in the pouring down rain,
But Lewis won't fall down, he will gain,
He acts different now, struggling to keep the ball, to stand up tall,
Wiping his once blond hair out of his face, stuck down, wet,
But Lewis won't give up, no, not yet,
Game over, we won,
'How do you do it?' I ask him, with a little grin,
'I never give up,' he replies.

Stacey Roberts (12)
Ifield Community College

Closest 2 God

It's our diary, it keeps our secrets.
It makes us happy when we are sad.
It makes us see when we are blind.
It's a pair of guidelines to help us through life.
It's our leader, the one we can trust.
It's our family, it's always there for us.
It's the one I love.

Courtni Gurd & Danielle Hunter (12)
Ifield Community College

When Lightning Comes

Terrifying, traumatic, tremendous, lightning is,
My friend is terrified and she's called Liz,
Like a dazzling stroke of sunlight,
It is so, so bright,
It's tremendous,
It's horrific,
It's like a big Ocean Pacific.

When it ends, my friend jumps high,
High, high up to the sky,
She's so pleased,
She automatically beams,
But then suddenly she cries,
I lied,
I love lightning,
Goodbye!

Alice Merle (11)
Ifield Community College

Creepy Crawlies

A dark, black ball
The long, loose threads
Coming out the side
The staring, black beads

A shiver down your spine
Creepy crawlies
One, two, three
There it goes
Catch it quick

Get a glass
Get a book
Grab the thing
Throw it out
There it goes.

Stephanie Harris (13)
Ifield Community College

The Ballad Of The Evil Lord

Once, long ago, there was an evil lord,
Who threatened his people with an iron sword,
The people were scared of what he might do,
If they did wrong, he would run them through.

No justice was seen, no justice was done,
Who would help them? They had no one,
Then one dark night a stranger came,
To fight the lord in their name.

Justice was served, justice was seen,
It was the happiest day that had ever been,
But the power was too much for him
And the people threatened to cut off his limb.

Down with the king, down with the sword,
They want no one to be their lord,
That was the day they had their own way,
Now they are all truly gay.

If you cheat and lie,
Your people can make you die,
If you treat people with respect,
The people will not neglect.

Luke Speakman (12)
Ifield Community College

Tornado

Its twisting acceleration.
Its multi-tonal colour.
Slowly whipping and winding
Like a train journey.
It seeks to destroy.
Lets no one stand in its way.
Destroying instinctively.
Destination undecided.
It's like an indecisive traveller
Destroying paths for itself.

Sean Reynolds (13)
Ifield Community College

A Nonsense Poem!

A flying elephant,
A pounding bird,
A fish on land,
A camel in water,
A cat barking,
A dog miaowing,
A blue sun,
An orange sea,
A round square,
A square circle,
A cup of food,
A piece of tea,
A zoo of people,
A house of animals,
A garden of books,
A library of flowers,
A stripy giraffe,
A spotty zebra,
A college of babies,
A nursery of adults.

Hollie Brandrick (11)
Ifield Community College

The End Of The World

The car light's blinding,
The fireplace's crackling,
The bonfire's roaring,
Rocks plummeting.

You can run, but not hide,
It sees all,
Turning on the lights,
Crowds shouting,
Lights out . . .

Forever!

Jackson Clarke (13)
Ifield Community College

Enter To Pray

I was sort of hoping
that you would come along
like the answer to a player
and the music to a song

Like the kind of things that happen
at a special place and time
that will change our lives forever
like a fantasy of mine

I still remember
when your lips first met mine
I felt alive

So pardon, if I look at you
forgive me if I stare
at the fantasy I knew before
I saw you standing there

What I was hoping for
it came along
like the answer to a player
and the music to a song.

Laeek Ahmed (13)
Ifield Community College

A Day Of Nonsense!

One October afternoon,
In the middle of July,
The snow was falling from the ground
And the flowers grew in the sky.
Yesterday it was freezing hot
And today it's baking cold.
I went down to the attic,
While my mum was up in the cellar.
Today is a very normal day,
You should see what it's like when it's
A day of nonsense.

Katie Everett (11)
Ifield Community College

My Guinea Pig

My guinea pig is so cute,
She's black and white
And fluffy.
She rolls around in the hay,
Trying to hide from me,
I go and feed her every night
And she squeaks and squeaks and squeaks.
I cover her up when it's cold
And when it's raining,
I do not want her to get cold,
Oh no, oh no, oh no.
She nibbles at her carrot,
As loud as can be,
She's always running wild,
That's how I know she's OK.
My guinea pig is so sweet,
I could hold her all day long,
She is so energetic.
I love my guinea pig so much,
She is the best!

Zoë Smith (13)
Ifield Community College

The Soaring Dragon

The dragon looking as hot as volcano lava,
She soars into the early evening sky,
The sun still shining bright and orange,
The sun making her skin shine in the exotic light,
She looks more beautiful than ever,
She even looks like the sun, so bright and beautiful,
She's so stunning and absolutely fabulous,
She's the best of the best,
She's the dragon . . . the lava dragon.

Kerry Leanne Weston (11)
Ifield Community College

Hallowe'en Misfortune

Hallowe'en is for scaring all of your friends
But something bad is happening
The ghouls won't get out of bed
And the skeletons are scared to even look in a mirror.

The zombies are locked in the graveyard
Down in their graves
The ghosts would help them
But they're not very brave.

The devils are in Hell
With all the naughty children
And the vampires aren't feeling well
Because they have the flu.

So for Hallowe'en you will have to make do
With all the little children dressing up
To go trick or treating with you.
Ha, ha, ha, ha!

Charlotte Hawes (11)
Ifield Community College

Guess Who?

A long swing hanging from the trees.
An acrobat running fast.
The sea-shaped banana.
A never-ending open book.
A loud radio.
A chair in the trees.
A furry brown cat's ball.
A clown with fleas.
A hamster in its wheel.
Guess who?

Elleana Piller (12)
Ifield Community College

Seasons - Haikus

Spring
Still a bit cold now
But the rabbits are bouncing
Happily and calm.

Summer
Sitting in the sun
And playing and having fun
In the paddling pool.

Autumn
Harvest is coming
Animals hibernating
The leaves are falling.

Winter
The snow is falling
We are decorating now
For Christmas is here!

Melissa Pitts (11)
Ifield Community College

The Sun

The sun is a huge beach ball floating round an endless sea,
It is an abandoned coin on an old road,
It is a burning fire on deserted land,
It is a fried egg with the yolk oozing out on a blue plate,
It is a light too bright to look at,
It is fine silk falling from the sky,
It is an orange plate covered by a cloud of steam,
A golden knob of butter in a hot pan,
That is the sun.

Charlotte Salmon (11)
Ifield Community College

Boys

I just can't understand
Why boys act like they do,
They are always playing football,
Is that all that they will do?
They never stop to look at the marvellous big wide world,
But the one thing that I *really* hate,
Is the way they treat us girls.

Us girls, on the other hand,
Are the best that we can be,
We always stop to take a look at any plant we see.

Now there's one more thing I have to say,
Before you turn the page,
I hope that if you are a boy,
You will think about your ways!

Claudia Spears (11)
Ifield Community College

Ice

A clear surface,
A cold point,
A slippy surface,
A shattering block,
A sun-reflecting barrier,
A frozen barrier,
An Eskimo's fishing place,
A polar bear's fun place,
A shattering god.

Michael Steers & Ross McDonald (12)
Ifield Community College

The Black Knight

The black knight riding along in pitch-black
It was windy and chilly and the leaves
Were flying across the road.
He rode up a gigantic hill and the horse
Just gave up and he fell.
He would lie there till the sun would
Rise and then he would walk again.

He walked throughout the day to find
His lady fair.
The moon was full and the wolves were
Howling when he walked to find his
Lady fair.
From the burning tower and until
He finds his lady fair, he will never
Rest again.

Gareth Biddle (13)
Ifield Community College

What Am I?

A huge bouncy castle
A huge paint spill
The sky's great moon
What am I?

A gleam of light
A game of splat that moves
A big ball of wool
What am I?

A big pile of fluff
A child's first picture
A lovely piece of candyfloss
What am I?

Bobby Harris (13)
Ifield Community College

The Happiness In The Seasons

The wind whipping in my face, being hot and gentle,
The waves lapping over each other, reminding me of kittens at play,
The sand smooth and wet against the soles of my feet,
The sensation of running on a lonely beach.
That makes me smile.

The force of children's feet, kicking the golden leaves,
The sunset in the evening, making the clouds pink,
The toasted marshmallows tingling my taste buds,
The sight of frost on the grass, making it sparkle.
That makes me smile.

The footprints in the snow, being bigger rather than smaller,
The way I can make snow angels on the cold ground,
The thought of having a snowman friend,
The feel of snowflakes in my hair.
That makes me smile.

The thought of waking up to the birds making melodies,
The sight of farm animals giving birth,
The helping of planting daffodil bulbs and watching them flower,
The watching of the bluebells, blowing in the wind.
That makes me smile.

But having a great time with my family and friends,
Whatever the season,
Is what makes me smile the most.

Abigail Reed (11)
Ifield Community College

Guess Who?

A jellyfish sting that doesn't go away.
A blood spill that stains your shirt.
A rose thorn that's stuck in your finger.
A scar forever, that you wish would go away.
A deep, bloody cut, dripping with blood.
A sharp, running pain, running down your spine.

Shanice Hersey (12)
Ifield Community College

Billy's Big Dream

Galloping savagely along the stream,
The raging horseman is never to be seen.
Like a cheetah at speed, with the leaves blowing high,
Whilst the barn owls glide high in the sky.

Going so fast, it's as if *he* can fly,
Then he stops like a bolt, with a great big sigh.
'I'm getting quite bored,' he said to himself,
As he sets off again and meets Jack the elf.

He trotted along, with Jack on the back,
A few minutes later, they were under attack.
There was *no need* to panic, luckily for them,
As it was their dear old friend, Goosy the hen.

Billy woke up crying his eyes out,
Whining and screaming, shout, shout, shout!
His mum calms him to go back to sleep,
Two seconds later, he was out like a bleep.

Lewis Williams (12)
Ifield Community College

I'm Your Nightmare

A breeze of broken ice,
A housekeeper,
A day off school,
A whisk,
A wind maker,
A whirlpool,
A Hoover,
A runner with one leg,
A digger,
A bully,
A never-ending hole.

Jessica Browne (12)
Ifield Community College

The Graveyard

It is scary
It's frightening
You would not want
To be there in the dark.

It is cold and misty
Bells ring 12 o'clock
Churches are being used
For praying by the dead.

It's gruesome
Rolling eyeballs on the ground
Spiders and cockroaches all over
Skeletons spitting
Trees shaking in the wind.
Where are you?

J'aime Luvin (12)
Ifield Community College

My Baby Brother

My baby brother is two years old,
He never does what he is told,
He walks and talks
And cries a lot,
But when he sleeps,
You come and see,
A different baby,
So warm and sleek,
He dreams of treats
And so many sweets.
That's when he awakes,
And he shouts,
'Yipee!'

Jade Ward (12)
Ifield Community College

A Tree

If I were a leaf upon a tree
Then I would live quite happily
I'd grow quite flat and green and big
Unless, of course, I was a twig.

But if I were a twig with a leaf on its end
Then the leaf would surely be my friend
And the leaf would come to count on me
To keep it visible, to see.

And if I were a long, strong branch
Then everyone would surely glance
I'd hold my twig and leaf with pride
And set myself aside.

But if I were the trunk of the great oak tree
Then branch, twig and leaf would surely be
All through the seasons, part of me
For I am the trunk of the great oak tree.

Tyler Anderson (12)
Ifield Community College

Little Kitten

Bursting out of the cage, like a volcano blowing its top,
Out came the kitten, thinks he is all innocent.
He's getting wound up, ready to pop,
Falling over his new legs, as if they're not his.
Learning to fight, scratching our fingertips,
Food time now, we are piling it on.
Kitten likes that sound, he is licking his lips.
Falling like a leaf, he has to stop for a while.

It's dark now, everyone is in bed,
Kitten's down, dreams running through his head.

Kyle Tansley (13)
Ifield Community College

Earthkeepers

Present at the birth of all,
Keepers of the knowledge of the universe,
These are the Earthkeepers.

Older than trees,
Wiser than owls,
Buried deep beneath us,
The Earthkeepers are.

Never to see the world,
Or the beauty of the night,
Yet they know . . .
And the creation of life,
They witnessed.

Many years ago,
When the world was fresh,
They breathed the air,
Glittered in the sun
And gazed at the stars
Of the evening sky.

Beneath the dirt
They now stay,
Away from the world
And the animals in it,
Waiting in silence,
Until the time has come
For them to rise again.

Violet Jarman (14)
Ifield Community College

Kitten

Soft bundle of fur, rolling round on the floor.
Frisky and lively, scurrying around the soft rug.
Back and forth, the bundle rolls out the door.
But I know she'll be back for even more.

Constance Crowhurst (12)
Ifield Community College

My Puppy's Gone

His golden-brown fleecy coat,
Shone in the sun,
When someone saw him in the street,
Smiles came to everyone.

Playing fetch and kicking the ball,
Were his favourite games,
We didn't know what to call him,
He really needed a name!

When we said, 'Fetch!' he'd run along
Barking very loud,
When I look up in the sky,
I see him in the clouds.

As I'm telling you this story,
I feel he's here with me,
Because he was very special,
So see you soon, RIP.

Jessica Harms (12)
Ifield Community College

Unicorn

There she goes - *flash!*
You missed her 'cause she made a dash.
I see her, she's cool,
If you can't see her, you're a fool.
Her body shimmers like the water,
But you can only find her if you are a daughter.
She runs about without a care,
Her mane and tail are white and fair.
Her life carries on like an unstoppable cart,
She is beautiful and strong, especially her heart.

Nicole Evans (13)
Ifield Community College

I Love My Little Brother

I love my little brother,
I think he's really cool,
But whenever we got out to tea,
He always acts the fool.

I love my little brother,
But he can be a pain,
One day he took my favourite bear
And threw it in the rain.

I love my little brother,
He always gets his way,
He can get me into trouble,
But I never get my say.

I love my little brother,
His mess, it is knee deep,
I still love my little brother,
Especially when he's asleep!

Kimberley Jones (14)
Ifield Community College

Newborn Kitten

As he stands up for the first time,
This tiny bundle of fur takes his first steps,
Little legs shaking,
Following his mum around everywhere she goes,
Wanting to be fed along the way,
Eyes watching everything,
Little legs shaking,
He loses his balance,
His mum is always there to help him.

Rebecca Cumbers (13)
Ifield Community College

Unicorn

There once was a unicorn
Named Mel
And around her neck hung a bell
So that whenever she moved
Would play a beautiful tune.

She had fur like snow
A mane like fire
And a point on the end of her horn.

But one terrible day
When she slept at the bay
She lost her golden bell.

She asked all around
If they'd seen her gold bell
But all they said was, 'Sorry Mel!'

When she got home
She saw something glistening galore
On her big forest floor.

She thought, *silly me*
As she remembered she had forgotten to wear her golden bell
She cried, 'Happy day!
I didn't lose my bell at the bay!'

William Ford (12)
Ifield Community College

The Winter Beach

Like a deserted heaven is the winter's beach,
The strong winds blowing you back and forwards,
The great smell of sea air
And the high waves thrashing against the beach,
The high screech of the seagulls,
At the beach in winter.

Lewis Breach (12)
Ifield Community College

My Little Sister

In the sweetness of dreamland, the baby sleeps,
Breathing gently - can't even speak,
Her head moves slowly as I sit on the floor,
I've never had a little sister before,
Mum's asleep too and so is Dad,
She's like a toy I've never had,
Okay, I admit, she's not that bad,
But when she cries, she makes me sad,
She soon wakes up with a tear and a roar,
I don't think she's in dreamland anymore,
I pick her up and hold her close,
She stops crying and still feels morose.
I lay her down in her cot,
I'm not tired, no I'm not,
She falls asleep and is back in dreamland again,
I should pay a visit there, I wonder when?

Louise Bliss (12)
Ifield Community College

The Baby

In his cot the baby sleeps for hours
His eyes are regularly closed up tight,
Only about four times a day
Does he awake to see daylight.

Mum and Dad are always there
They rock the cradle to and fro,
When poor baby always cries
His parents always come and go.

They want to wrap him up all nice and warm
So they can take him out in his pram,
With comfort of his tiny thumb
He's always asleep like a little, fluffy lamb.

Hollie Stacey (12)
Ifield Community College

Saturday Night Fight

The reigning heavyweight champion of the world,
In this fantastic title fight.
By the winner, the belt will be held,
This will prove to be an eventful night.

Out comes the contender,
Raring to go.
A challenge to the defender,
Who will win? No one knows.

The fighters jump straight in,
The fight continues, as they boost the pace.
Both fighters knowing, the loser will be left in the bin,
Totally ashamed, afraid to show their face.

Then it happened, you could hear the crunch,
The bone-shattering smash.
The champion went down from the almighty punch,
As he hit the floor with a crash.

Seven, eight, nine, ten,
The champion had suffered defeat.
Would he get the title again?
The challenger taunted, 'You're dead meat!'

Michael Roberts (12)
Ifield Community College

Phoenix

P hoenix with their hot bodies, their flaming tails,
H ot, the phoenix dies, only to be reborn as an egg,
O range and red with flaming feathers and its hot breath,
E ach day rules the sky, the phoenix is a gentle bird,
N ear its death it makes a nest on ashes to burn,
 I ts death is not so bad, as it still lives on as a new one,
X marks the spot, you lay and rest.

Roxanne Davey (12)
Ifield Community College

The Ballad Of The Candle

The building was falling
People were dying
Women were calling
Children were crying.

The building was 100 feet tall
They were in great danger
The only way to get down was
All they needed was a ranger.

They could not see the light
They wanted to get out
The men used all of their might
All were trying to shout.

They shouldn't have lit the fire
There wouldn't have been a disaster
Which they could not handle
And never had to pick-up after.

Do not play with fire
If you do
This will happen to you
Don't play with fire.

Eddie Edge (12)
Ifield Community College

What Am I?

As high as the wind
As low as the land
Catches its prey with a swipe of its hand.
It can fly to an island
On an endless trail
I can also deliver mail.
What am I?

I'm a delivery pigeon.

Jasmine Hunn (12)
Ifield Community College

The Big Bang

One gloomy day in London City
There was a man in such a pity;
He had to accuse a working man,
Who did something bad.

It occurred in the month of May
That Mr Carn had to say
'Sorry, you're sacked,
I have to say.'

'Farewell, my dear man
I have to say, that you must
Leave the building right now
Never to darken these doors again!'

The night was full of gloom,
When he went to his room
He decided to plant a bomb
In the building he'd come from.

He went outside and waiting another 30 seconds,
Everyone heard a big bang;
He ran into the building to save his dear friends
But it was too late, he was coughing so much
That he couldn't get out himself.

Leanne Ford (12)
Ifield Community College

The Puppy

He has a very weak bark
His name is Mark,
He makes a mess
We brought him from Loch Ness.

He scampers round the house
Running away from a little mouse,
He howls through the night.

Conor Phillips (12)
Ifield Community College

Wintertime!

Winter is coming,
It's already here.
Do you know what that means?
It's Christmas time!

Let's decorate the tree,
Cover it with tinsel.
Baubles and bubbles,
Kisses and cuddles.

It stands there,
Like the star on its head,
Shimmery and glittery.
It's awesome!

Presents sit under the branches,
All different shapes and sizes.
There's a bike and a ball!
Here's a new swimming pool!

We trudge outside,
With our scarves and our hats,
Our coats done up tightly,
Leaving in snow, our tracks.

Snowmen grow,
Snowballs get thrown.
Splat! One hits me on the head,
So I throw one back.
Ha! Ha!

Winter is going,
It's already gone.
Do you know what that means?
No more Christmas!

Eloisa Mae Gordon (12)
Ifield Community College

The Undiscovered World

As the sun, above the hill,
Rises and shines,
The water, drop by drop,
Crashes in a noisy mist,
It tumbles down
And hides an undiscovered world,
From which emerges
A beautiful creature:
The unicorn,
Who is alive and real,
But is merely a dream,
As faint as a sleeping
Child.

Alexandra Craven (12)
Ifield Community College

Winter Day

Summer's gone, winter's here,
It's that cold time of year,
Zip up your coat to keep nice and warm,
During the rain and during the storm,
Sit at the fireplace on winter nights,
Don't go out or you'll get frostbite!

Winter is cold, but can be fun,
Throwing snowballs, to laugh and to run,
To slip and to slide on the slippery ice,
To make snowmen, it's utter delight,
But as the sun peeps through the clouds,
The white snow and frosty ice disappear . . .
Until next time!

Kelly Wheller (12)
Ifield Community College

The Beach In Winter

The beach was chilly
The wind chattered,
The boys were being silly
As the rocks got battered.

The tide was coming in
As the waves climbed
Up the stones and near the bin
The beach began to shine.

The boys mucked around
As the tide ate one,
He was nowhere to be found
So much for a day full of fun.

Their hearts sank like a ship
Suddenly, their mums appeared,
The boys all bit their lips
He might have floated near the pier.

They ran as if on fire
Their mums screaming behind them,
They knew they would be a liar
Maybe he'd come back but when?

A few months had gone
The boy had been found,
It was shown when a news document came on
Benny's mum frowned.

Too right it was him
Washed up on the shore,
Benny did a bad sin
The little boy was only four.

Amber Henley (12)
Ifield Community College

The Unicorn And The Griffin

There was once a griffin, whose fur was as red as vermilion.
There was also a unicorn, whose mane was as clear as ice.
They lived in peace and harmony.
Until that fateful day.

The storm was brewing,
One winter's eve
The unicorn asked the griffin
'Can you find a shelter for me?'

And so the griffin got ready to fly,
Up, up, he went singing on the way,
Until he suddenly struck upon
A shelter for the unicorn.

It was a little cave,
On a little hillside,
As he turned back,
Crack he got hit on the back.

Down and down he fell,
Faster and faster, he grew nearer to the ground,
With a thud
He smacked the ground.

The unicorn, who was grazing nearby,
Happened to hear the thud
And so she ran in the direction
That it came from.

So she ran at the speed of an Olympic runner,
Then, as the whistling wind,
Until she saw her friend the griffin
With a bruise on his wing.

'Did you find the shelter?' she said,
'Yes, over there, not far,' he replied
So she helped the griffin onto her back
And she ran as fast as she could.

Finally, she reached the opening
She was glad
She knelt down to let the griffin rest
And from that day onwards
They were soulmates till the end.

Toby Bassett (12)
Ifield Community College

The Black Pearl

On a dark, lightless night
The HMS Bishop sliced through the ocean
When the lookout shouted, 'Ahoy! Ahoy!'
The captain, he did run to see the Black Pearl.

The cannon men did fire
But missed and struck the night
The Pearl fired back
And destroyed the nest.

The Black Pearl rammed the HMS Bishop
They could not run, they just sunk
As it was sinking
The Pearl's men raided the treasure.

As the men jumped back on to the pearl
They heard a deafening *bang!*
The men swung round, with treasure in hand
The captain shouted, 'You are damned to Hell!'
The men, they did chuckle.

As daylight came, the men were as tired as ever
They tried pulling the sails up
But the pulleys were rusted
The men were stuck in the middle of the ocean.

A cannon man ran up
'There's a hole in the side of the ship!'
The Black Pearl was sinking
The men were beaten by the ocean.

Sam Walsh (12)
Ifield Community College

Family

In our family,
Dad is the fizz in Coke,
He's a pair of faded jeans,
He's a flying football always moving
And he's the sun after a heavy thunderstorm.

In our family,
Mum is a hot tumble-dryer, drying the washing,
She is the crunch in the autumn leaves,
She's the happiness when you feel scared
And she is the, 'Go to bed,' when you wish it could be, 'Stay up.'

In our family,
Ben is the bubbles in a bubbly chocolate bar,
He's your favourite pair of jeans,
He is the winning drop goal in the rugby World Cup final
And he's the thunder in a storm.

In our family,
Hannah is the kitchen sink splashing water,
She is the laughter in a funny film,
She's the cold in the winter, but warmth in the summer
And she's the, 'Hello,' in your bedroom when you wish it was 'Bye.'

In our family,
That leaves me
And I'm
Not telling!

Abby Winter (12)
Ifield Community College

My Little Sister

My little sister is a pain,
Moaning, crying again and again,
She won't do anything for herself,
She stands there waiting for someone else,
The only time I get some peace,
Is when she's lying there, fast asleep.

Katie Davey (12)
Ifield Community College

What Am I?

What am I?
Golden yolk on a blue plate,
An orange balloon,
A golden coin in the sky,
An orange in darkness,
A golden-headed child,
A light bulb,
The everlasting light.

What am I?
A pile of rubbish,
The natural home
Of our ancestors,
Deserted or
Full,
Life is common,
Tragedy happens,
Good or bad,
Separated forever,
Survivor,
Immortal.

Danielle Louise Fisher (11)
Ifield Community College

Charlie

Tight, blond curls brush along my arm,
As he wriggles in his sleep.
He is waking up,
He stretches and slowly pulls himself up,
Opening his sparkly, sea-blue eyes.
He sees his train,
He crawls into the middle of the room.
He grabs it and cuddles it,
He lays down and falls back to sleep.

Sophie Waters (12)
Ifield Community College

When I'm With You

When I'm with you,
I feel just fine.
Especially to know that you're all mine!
I think about you every morning,
When I'm not with you, everything is boring.
You are my life,
My one true love.

When I'm with you,
You make me smile.
Even if it's just for a little while.
You are my passion, my one desire,
Our relationship burns,
Like a flame in a fire.

I wrote this poem to give you a clue,
That I am nothing
Without you.

Nicola Barton (14)
Ifield Community College

My Sister

My sister is the most beautiful creature you'd ever see.
When she comes in the room, your eyes fill with glee.
Her silky hair and pale, soft skin.
Her waddling legs make her glide with the wind.
She looks at you and her eyes light up with fire.
When she plays her game and likes to hide
Be sure she'll give you a fright,
But the inner angel of my sister
Will be sure that you won't miss her.
When she sleeps, she's as quiet as a mouse
And even though we love her, she often rules our house.

Aron Jacob (12)
Ifield Community College

Tornado

A tornado rips and tears as it spins
It tears things down as it passes through villages
It is a very powerful wind
No one and nothing can stop it.
It spins so fast, if you get in its way it will blow you away.
It rips through houses and trees like matchboxes.
Everything it touches falls to the ground;
The only way to get away from it, is to run the other way
It's spinning.
It picks things up as it's spinning for miles
Lets them go and they go flying to the ground,
It looks like torn feathers and confetti.
It sounds like a massive roar and a really loud blowing sound.
All you can do is watch it smashing
Things and tearing things down
As it passes through to go to its next place.

Jamie Finch (15)
Ifield Community College

Puppy At Home

I woke up the 3 month old puppy from his bed,
When he was born, I called him Ted.
Ted likes to run, Ted likes to play,
I'll take him to the garden and he'll play all day.

I bought him a tennis ball,
Ted cutely rolls it; compared to him, it's tall.
When I look into Ted's eyes I see the sea
And I know how peaceful life can be.

Ted my puppy, I'll never let you go,
Because soon you'll be in a show.
And I'll let you know, I'll always love Ted,
Even when he snuggles off to bed.

Sarah Greenan (12)
Ifield Community College

Nothing

Good friends, nothing more
Your words ring in my head.
Nothing more, nothing more
Haunt me while I lay in bed.
I wish I had seen it coming
I really wish I knew
How to save myself from this heartache
And the tears that I cry for you.
It's not like I'm so perfect
And you have your flaws too
But nobody could take away
These feelings that burn for you.
They said we were great together
And that we should never part
But as I stare at you, so near, yet so far
Who knew you could break my heart?
It's silly really, I shouldn't care
At least we'll always be friends
Good friends, that's it, nothing more
Good friends and nothing less.

Danielle Didcock (15)
Ifield Community College

Dwelling On A Fantasy

I dream of a creature of innocence and purity
Disillusioned by this creature of hallucinating beauty
It seems to me an untouchable fantasy
If only I could lose myself in its phantom captivity
And escape this world of tedious tendencies
While denying myself of inane insecurities
Protecting self-worth from darkness and monotony
Shielding myself from hurt and hostility
Avoiding anger eating my reality until my life
Has been wasted dwelling on this fantasy.

Sohpie Dowdeswell (17)
Ifield Community College

You

I lie here asleep
I wait for happiness so I can weep
But I can't find happiness where I am
I drown my sorrows as if there is no tomorrow
Why do I feel so blue?
I wonder if I should love you -
There are doors shut with glue.

The poison is in my veins
It's taking over me
It's not just a game
You laugh as I'm in pain
I lay here in fear
How did I get here?
Many whispers stirring on and on.

I sit here and think
While depressing songs fill my mind
Those sorrowful words
I beg myself not to fall
But I can't walk, I just crawl.

My life is destroyed, I'm trying to avoid
But my mind is shut with glue
Closed like a hut
All the heartache
There is no escape
My mind crumbles
The dark hour is here
I'm on my own but in a crowded room
Where are you now?

You were my love, but you are less cunning
I'm running
From you!

Kerrie Bailey (15)
Ifield Community College

I Hate Cheese

I so really hate
When it's on my plate
This thing called cheese
It makes me sneeze
Be cold or hot
I'll be off like a shot
If it's a slice
It's still not nice
Even grated
No . . . still not rated!
When it's on toast
It makes me roast
Soft or hard
I'm on my guard
It makes me sick
And gets on my wick
It smells of feet
And it's not a treat
I just hate cheese
So . . . no thank you, please.

Jamie Saunders (13)
Ifield Community College

Bloody Forest

Deafening wolf-like howls of pain
Capture the blood-soaked air
Swarms of angry arrows fire
From the limb-lined trees.

The vermilion men absorb their last seconds
Of cascading pain, the scavenging, cowardly vultures
Pick off the weak and injured . . . brave, struck down, lions.

Swords dive into cracking and tearing flesh and bone
The howling dies down, along with the brave warriors
Encouraged by their determination, which had also wavered.

Daniel Gray (13)
Ifield Community College

The Dog Who Had His Way

Two dogs went out one day,
Into the farmyard to play in the hay.
The first dog said, 'Let's go scare the pig!'
The second dog said, 'She will give you a dig!'

But the first dog didn't listen
And went to scare the pig!
And of course, she gave him a dig!
There was a yelp and a crash and a bark and a *bash!*

The second dog said, 'That was what I warned!'
The first dog limped as if he had been burned.
So the second dog took the first dog home
And they sat by the fire with a juicy bone.

Don't try to scare someone
When you know it's going to backfire!

Natasha Barwise (12)
Ifield Community College

The Chestnut Tree

The chestnut tree, old and sleek,
When it falls, it will make you weep,
Twenty-foot high, it will make you sigh.

But when it falls, people will open their doors and cry,
'The chestnut tree has fallen,
Go and get the Community Warden.'

But then, silence, the five-year-old is planting another one,
Soon it will be higher than the sun and the sky.

The little one will say, 'This is mine, the only one.
It started off as big as my thumb,
But when it grows, everyone will say, *hooray!'*

Adam Nelson (13)
Ifield Community College

Santa Got Macarooned

I was sitting in the fortune tent,
Listening, as quiet as could be,
When she answered me
Eventually,
She sounded quite possessed
And yet my life is still clouded in mystery.

Spontaneously, she grabbed my throat
And made it really sore.
She chucked me out,
Into the drought,
So fast, I could not
Grab my coat.

When I finally came back to a halt,
My mind was still up there,
I could not grab it back,
My body shrivelled to an awkward position
In the cold, blue air.

That was when I decided to make my life worthwhile
I stopped to think,
I paused to think,
In a little pile,
That was when it struck me;
You know that wonderful idea,
I know, I'll be Santa Claus!

So, that night, I hired a herd of huge reindeer,
To help me with my jingle round - each and every year
Until I retired
And until their dates expired.
So, I flew off, up in my sleigh
On each Christmas Eve.

Until of course
I flew off course
And began to swing and sway
And then when I looped the loop

I slipped and lost a tray,
Until back when on course
I realised that
I'd had too much chardonnay!

So that night I buckled down
The reindeer worked hard too
Then that night
There came a fright
The parents they did frown
When I fell down the wrong chimney
And landed in the loo!

So shameful,
How embarrassing,
I thought to myself,
I'm flying in Cape Baboon,
When suddenly my sleigh, it crashed
The cannibals hurried to the scene
So that's *how I got macarooned!*

Charlie Jones (12)
Ifield Community College

Death

An eclipse,
The end of the line,
The last straw,
A light at the end of a tunnel,
The gates opening,
A scythe,
A voice,
A giant hand reaching for you,
No more chances.

Jack Peevor (13)
Ifield Community College

Power Of Nature

The man said it was coming
I was sitting there humming
Find a place, find a space
How and behold we
Stayed low.

Outside things are flying
People are frying
Oh, God help us
Say us, pray, pray, pray
Close your eyes and hope
It sounded like a twister
Sucking up like a vacuum cleaner
But leaving its destroyed toys behind
Rain, rain over our heads
Glass smashed, cars bashed
Houses flat as a mat
Trees fall like raindrops.

Pick up the pieces
One by one, brick by brick
Help is at hand on this troubled land
Peace for now.

Usman Sarwar (15)
Ifield Community College

Spaghetti

Swirly, slimy, yummy spaghetti
Sliding down my throat
Sometimes it is smelly and wiggly
Just like a worm that's gross.
Spaghetti, spaghetti how slidy and gross
You seem smelly and soft
You're just like a snake
You slither and slide
When you eat it you fly.

Rebecca Cooper (11)
Ifield Community College

The Shining Sun

The scorching, sizzling, shining sun
Shining down on me
I am running around, up and down
As happy as can be.

10am and the sun is still rising,
Rising like a bird,
Over the city, over the streets,
Shining round the Earth,
Never-ending light,
How I wish that could be,
Having the sun,
Burning bright,
For all eternity.

The scorching, sizzling, shining sun
Shining down on me
I am running around, up and down
As happy as can be.

1pm and the sun is so high,
More than a thousand metres in the sky,
Like a circular cloud,
Orange and yellow,
Looking up makes me feel mellow.

The scorching, sizzling, shining sun
Shining down on me
I am running around, up and down
As happy as can be.

After 5pm the sun is setting,
Sinking slowly as can be,
Behind the mountains it disappears,
Out of view from me,
The sky changes colour as I walk away,
Hoping for another sunny day.

Jason Raj (14)
Ifield Community College

Kittens

Its gaze so soft and full of devotion
It walks in slow motion
Slinking towards a bird, sleeping
The bird awakes and flies off
It miaows as if it were weeping.

Its fur so soft, silky and white
That even the sun and moon
Stop and stare.

As it curls up on your lap,
You can feel how much it cares.
The only creature this could be
Is a sweet and gentle *kitten!*

Maria Rowsell (12)
Ifield Community College

The Unicorn

I was there, at morning daybreak, looking out so sea,
Within the streets, chattering way beside me,
I overheard about a creature coming in
When I looked over my shoulder,
I saw the creature behind me.

The creature was as white as snow,
The creature's horn was as gold as a tablet in a treasure chest,
The crowd asked, 'What is it?'
I said, 'I had no notion of what is was!'

I will never know!

Danielle Louise Pay (12)
Ifield Community College

Sky

A huge, blue duvet cover
A smeared painting
A huge, deep swimming pool.

A moaning grandpa
A thumping rabbit
A huge flash of light
A dark night.

A pinky-purple picture
An orange carpet
A slate of blue ice.

Claire Hewitt (13)
Ifield Community College

Silent In The Library

Silent in the library,
You can hear a pin drop,
I hate it when it's quiet,
It gets me in a strop.

No noise here, no noise there,
Everyone is busy,
I hate that there's no noise in here,
And I am starting to feel dizzy.

I wish everybody would be loud,
I wish they would stop working hard,
Am I the only one that's not a brainbox?
I might as well be made of card.

Come on children, let's start talking,
I'm fed up with no noise,
Why can't we all start screaming and laughing?
Come on girls and boys!

Maisie McGuirk (11)
Lavant House School

Wild Horses

Running wild in the wind,
She gallops on and on with her friend,
Knowing where they want to go,
They canter fast, then walk slow.
They stop in a clearing,
Hearing,
Ears pricked, they rest.

Suddenly they have to gallop,
Jump over hedges,
Struggle through branches.
They hear a bang,
They look, their hearts stop.
The machines are going fast, the enemy is back,
Their trees are under attack!
They hide behind a stump,
Watch their home disappear
They know their home is gone,
Joy goes away, the horses shed a tear.

Hannah Martin (11)
Lavant House School

Being

Lying on my back
Grass swaying above me
Some leaves tripping down
I am listening, listening.

Sitting at the door
Wind whipping the tree's branches
Clouds racing above me
I am looking, looking.

Standing on the grass
Watching the sunset sky
Hearing a fox barking
I am living, living.

Chloë Keir Watson (11)
Lavant House School

Two Men

(This is dedicated to everyone who has been held hostage over the war in Iraq or after it.)

Wondering what will happen,
If they will ever see tomorrow.
Wondering
If this is all just a lie.

Wondering if the light will turn on,
Will they ever be free?
Wondering
How is my family?

Waiting in anticipation,
To finally get a call,
Waiting in hope,
For you to walk through the door.

Waiting together,
Bruised all over,
Waiting for one chance,
One chance to be free.

What is happening to this world?
What started out as peace,
Has turned into mayhem.

We are sorry, brave men,
To put you through all this pain,
We hear your yells
Sentenced to death,
How do you keep going to the day?

Alone, where are you?
Where is everyone?
Oh yes, you're dead
Alone now you're gone.

Florence Christie (11)
Lavant House School

World War II

Bombs dropping all over the place
Hitler punishing people of a different race

Star badge of a Jew
Life in hiding is very new

Evacuees say goodbye
While trying not to cry

Hear the screaming of a kid
He must have run away and hid

The air raid's on
Where's that shop gone?

Gassed showers
Frightened for hours

Six years passed
And long they did last

Hitler's dead
His own bullet through his head

Britain's cheers
Drinking lots of beers!

Rebecca Richards (12)
Lavant House School

My Dog Rags

I used to have a dog called Rags,
She was my very best friend,
She was an unusual sort of dog,
But loving care she'd always lend.

She'd comfort me when I was scared,
And when I was feeling sad,
But now she's gone, I feel alone,
And so do Mum and Dad.

Suzanne Peckham (12)
Lavant House School

Fairytale

Cinderella lived happily ever after
Sleeping Beauty slept for one hundred years.
In fairytales, birds sing, but never die
Wicked things the princess never hears.
But hidden in the forests, buried in the ground,
Evil waits, plotting kindness's fate.
The princess hides her many sins.
The king has murder behind his smiles.
Stories are only stories after all,
You cannot wish on a star anymore,
You don't meet Prince Charming at any ball,
No one's perfect and we all have our flaws.
So don't open your book, but look into
Your heart, instead of through a glass, darkly.

Harriet Mullins (16)
Lavant House School

Epitaph For Youth

I plead to God to quiet their fearful cries,
Portraits of youth languishing in the dark.
Hell is nothing compared to those eyes,
Those still unseeing eyes that stop the heart,
Take away your breath and silence life.
But still a whisper is loud enough,
To hear these cries of buried strife.
Those who lost their lives in vain, we rebuff.
What right do we have to simply forget?
To lose in our sights and in our minds.
If our paths are chosen, already set,
Then God must know those eyes soon to blind.
Those who died fighting for their lives,
I for one shall never forget.

Louise Cavanagh (14)
Lavant House School

A Day With My Pony!

The sun was bright but it was still cold,
I was on my travels feeling bright and bold.
Wrapped up well I arrived at the yard,
My feelings today it was going to be hard.
Into our red trailer she had to go,
The journey took an age and seemed very slow.
Kizzy performed and behaved very well,
Then her mood changed and out broke hell.
She was stubborn and refused to jump,
My instructor was angry and said, 'Whip her rump.'
Tilly, my friend, lent me her pony, Jack,
She said she would be happy to ride Kizzy back.
Slightly disappointed on my journey home,
I think I need a new pony on loan.

Natalie Anscombe (14)
Lavant House School

Turkey!

It was hot, extremely hot,
I turned over and over,
I felt sticky and very sweaty from being in bed so long,
I opened my eyes, my mind,
It was morning.
The intoxicating smell of olive trees crept into my thoughts,
The sound the busy gecko makes raced in my ears,
The sight of sleeping bodies, swimming pools, mountains, hot sun,
                                                filled my mind.
I felt hot air, hot bed, soft carpet, cold tiles,
Then the reviving cold water trickling down my spine, in my hair,
                                                on my face.
I stepped outside to experience the wonderful sight of,
Olives, cheese, bread, honey, melon, figs and oranges,
I tasted,
Olives, cheese, bread, honey, melon, figs and oranges,
I drank icy cold water.

Ayesha Miles (14)
Lavant House School

Unknown Love

The love lingers on, his voice in my head
But now he lays there, peaceful, though dead.
The wondrous beat of his heart near is still
I feel no warmth in the day, but a chill.
The fear is gripping, the pain is like knives
All I want is for him to be alive.
I've wished too much, brought it on myself
And now I am surely condemned to Hell.
Life without him is hell to be sure,
I only wish I had been able to find a cure.
I feel I'm hitting my head with a brick,
I'll end my suffering it will be quick.
One drop of poison, a wound to my heart
Love is forever, 'til death do you part.

Molly Richard (14)
Lavant House School

Dear To Me

I woke up today at the crack of dawn,
Just to see a certain something on the lawn,
A fox and his mother were passing through,
But what would they find except morning dew?
Nothing, that's what, it was all quiet and still,
I sat there for hours; I had time to fill,
Watching and waiting for something to happen,
There was nothing, no where to go and that was apparent.

Then the sun came up gleaming through the trees,
I stood up and watched, I went weak at the knees,
Such a beautiful sight in the morning to see,
It reminds me of all the things I hold dear to me,
My love for my family, my friends and for all,
And that is just one thing no one should ignore.

Chloe Oecken (14)
Lavant House School

Known Too Late

The day my eyes broke open wide and true,
The day the song changed from old to brand new.
Your reflection, shining, scarring, engraved,
We were together, forever, never,
To be left alone, or have this feeling fade.

Time changed, but the feeling was not taken,
A chance, of us together, but forsaken,
Was the outcome of the end of something,
That once I thought was the beginning.
The end of our love, in death, together,
Forever, never to become broken.
The crowds of our cold disastrous fate:
My only love sprung from my only hate,
Too early seen unknown and known too late.

Harriet Elsom (14)
Lavant House School

Forgotten

Sitting alone in my room, I ask you
Why did you not listen, it was me you hurt too?
You loved me yet forgot me, you forgot you,
Like a shipwreck I was left to sink, you caused pain, destruction,
Everything shattering, crumbling around,
Did you not care, slipping, sliding into your depression?
Our relationship an iceberg; portrayed as two kinds, you hid away
                                            making no sound,
You let it take over, covering with your act,
But now you are gone, I cannot help you there,
I see now you were a child at heart, drowning in an adult's world,
I call out to you, I hear nothing back,
It's not the same without you, I miss you, I sit curled,
An empty feeling deep down inside, there's something we both lack,
I reach out desperate to hold on; it slips through my fingers like sand,
But you are gone, you are never coming back.

Charlotte Torr (14)
Lavant House School

Lavant House

Lavant House was founded
In nineteen-fifty-two
It then was West Lavant House
The pupils there were few!

Lavant House has grown now
It's gone from small to big
We have a lot of horses
We even had a pig!

Lavant is a nice school
As nice as nice could be
You can board at Lavant House
That's the place for me!

I go to Lavant House
Please let us win
My school need some hockey sticks
And a lovely new bin!

Marcia Miles (12)
Lavant House School

That Smile!

A twinkle in the eye,
A dimple in the cheek,
That smile was building up all week!

A jiggle of the shoulders,
A tremble of the lip,
That laugh could almost launch a ship!

An uncontrollable shake,
Tears running down my face,
That giggle's making me a nutcase!

A line of random words,
About to reach the punch line,
That joke was the funniest of my time!

Holly Edwards (11)
Lavant House School

Inside A Girl's Head

Dreams and wishes
Hugs and kisses
Pink clouds for me and for you
Stories of horses
Stories of ponies
How I wish they would all come true.

Days with my dogs full of sunshine and fun
Running on the beach it has to be done
Days of blue skies and good times to come
Days in midwinter full of snow and numb bums!

Days filled with friends all making me laugh
Evenings in front of a cosy hearth
Life is so good
Life is such fun
Oh how I wish it would go on and on.

Georgiana Upfold (12)
Lavant House School

Soothing Summers

I lay in my hammock,
Without a thought in my mind
Watching the clouds slide silently by.

Asleep by the sea
Waves lapping the shore
Feeling the sun calming my nerves.

Dreaming in a field
Full of pungent wild flowers
The smell soothing my senses.

These are all
Lazy, hazy summer days
That I wish could last forever.

Connie Chen (12)
Lavant House School

As I Walk Along The Beach

As I walk along the beach with the sea breeze in my hair, I gaze up at the sky and watch the seagulls fly under the fluffy candyfloss clouds.

The waves slowly floating until their time comes to an end and they violently crash up against the shingle and the remainder seeps back to the giant ocean.

As I make my way across the sand my temptation starts to grow, I undo my laces and slip off my shoes; I whip off my socks and run towards freedom.

I dash into the sea and feel the water amongst my toes, the seaweed rubs against my legs and I sink into the sand.

Then I run deeper and my feet lift off the floor.

My hair's down loose and gently flows as I dive down into the depths.

I go deeper and deeper, gliding like a fish, as I take my head above the water gasping for a breath, my mum and dad call me back in.

I dash out wrapping a towel around my waist and then I recline on the pebbles and have the lovely summer's picnic that we had all been waiting for, with my family.

Francesca Betes (12)
Lavant House School

A Poem About The Countryside

Our countryside can be peaceful,
And noisy.

Green fields and tall trees,
That whistle in the wind.

Squirrels are out and about in the fields,
Rabbits and badgers hop and look around for food.

Tractors come and plough our fields,
The farmers wearing their flat caps,
Looking after our countryside.

I love my countryside,
I hope it will always be there.

Amelia Hendy (12)
Lavant House School

Seasons

Winter's snow on the land below,
Flying in on the north wind's blow,
A sky so white with snowy might,
Covers the ground with icy light.

Spring arrives, the grass is green,
Flowers bloom for to be seen,
Along with trees with leaves so green,
That grow beside the little stream.

Summer's here with hot sea breeze,
And hayfever makes everyone sneeze,
There's not a cloud in the sky,
And all the land is burned dry.

Autumn comes in a glorious haze,
People say the best of days,
Farmers gather in the hay,
And the autumn gales begin to bay.

Alexandra Gibson (13)
Lavant House School

War Is Peaceful For England

For our country, England, war seems peaceful,
The distance acts like our nation's dimmer,
We try to silence the far off bombs' fall,
Only their candles stand as hope's glimmer.
Try to hide the slaughter of innocence,
Massacre their religion and cultures;
They're the children with no independence,
America is God; we are his vultures.
We have sent so many soldiers to serve,
That we lose count of how many we've lost,
But the nation finally grieves through dirge,
And war is brought home at a priceless cost.
'Two wrongs don't have a conclusion of right,'
So let's stop fighting and end Iraq's plight!

Daisy Christie (14)
Lavant House School

New Gift

From the moment you go in a shop,
To the moment you come out,
You know you're getting something new,
And you want to let out that shout.

Your mum lets you on the loose,
With a twenty dollar bill,
Your fingers tingle as you touch your gift,
And you can't wait to get to the till.

You and your mum all meet up,
And into the car you go,
You open your bag and look at your gift,
And want to put it on show.

When you get home it's time for bed,
You can't wait to begin a new day,
But then you get bored and ask your mum,
'Can I have something new to play?'

Alex Day (12)
Lavant House School

Summer Sensations

The summer sun beaming down so brightly
On the flowers in the meadow playing
Everything around is bright and sprightly
The donkeys inside the orchard braying
The clouds are floating in the sky above
The seagulls reeling in the peaceful sky
The entire world is filled with nature's love
The day goes peacefully and quietly by
Cracks of light above the tall, green tree tops
The deer and fawn graze by the water's side
A rabbit and her family quietly hops
When people come they run quickly to hide
In the tall damp woods, all is quiet and dark
Food is very little and life is stark.

Samantha Day (14)
Lavant House School

Where Are You Mum?

Where are you Mum on this frightful night?
There is no speck or glance of light,
Oh come on Mum, come soon,
All I can see is pitch black and the big dark moon.

I'm left here in the car park, can't you remember?
I don't want to be left here in late December,
There's not much light,
It's pitch black tonight.

As I whisper to and fro,
There are some things I'll never know,
Just then a crow goes whooshing by,
As I'm left here with a sigh.

These trees have claws and it's not very fair,
I just stand here and I glare,
This place is dark; it's giving me a fright,
Oh come on Mum, it's a Friday night.

I see a light,
Can it be?
It just might,
At last Mum is here,
To take away all my fear.

Jemma Simpson (11)
Lavant House School

My Fairy

I didn't hear a thing,
But she caught my eye.
She was like winter breath on a cold night.
She just fluttered around the moon's shadow,
Like a leaf that never managed to fall to the ground.
I took a step, but my fairy flew away,
I was so sad she had gone.
But maybe, just maybe she will come and visit me again.

Georgia Ellis (12)
Lavant House School

Goodbye

It's hard to say goodbye,
You wish the day would never come.

It's hard to say goodbye,
But when you have you're glad it's done.

It's hard to say goodbye,
Especially to a loved one.

It's hard to say goodbye,
But think of all the good times and fun.

It's hard to say goodbye,
But not for some, they're the lucky ones.

It's hard to say goodbye,
But don't take it for granted; be glad you had the chance.

It's hard to say goodbye,
But they wouldn't want you to shed a tear.

It's hard to say goodbye,
Look to the future and block out the fear.

It's hard to say goodbye,
These are the last lines.

It's hard to say goodbye,
But don't forget, remember the good times.

Chelsea Edmeads (14)
Longhill High School

Kitty Cats

Cats are scruffy, fluffy, cute and cuddly.
They're playful, graceful and rather funny.
They come in lots of shapes and sizes,
And when they smell food their tail rises.
I have two of my own and I wouldn't be without them.
They're more precious than rubies, diamonds or any other gem.

Emma Shahmir (12)
Longhill High School

Resist

Feelings of doubt fill my mind,
As he pulls me in with his staring eyes,
This has happened before,
This isn't a first,
My throat dries up,
It can only get worse,
A force drags me in,
My head starts to spin,
Do I want it or not,
I just do not know,
I try to pull back,
The force is too strong,
The way he stares,
It never stops,
I hate the way he has control,
I hate the way he drags me in,
I hate the way I cannot resist,
I cannot resist his tempting kiss.

Emily Adsett (14)
Longhill High School

Spring

Spring tiptoed into the summer holidays,
In the sandy beaches,
With a bright blue sky,
But never a word she said.

Spring settled by the calm sea,
Never making a wave,
Took a part of the sunset and then went dark.

Spring skipped down the month,
Never wanting to leave,
Along came summer wanting her to move.

Bethany Mitten (12)
Longhill High School

Running Away

If I were to run away,
I'd run away to sea,
But then again, after leaving my home,
What would become of me?

No one knows what lies out there,
Among those crested waves,
Maybe pirates, maybe smugglers,
Maybe captives and or slaves.

I might die out there alone
And only the wind would hear me crying,
With nobody to hold me close,
To stop me from dying.

But then again I might live,
To tell my tale,
About stormy seas and wonderful lands,
Smugglers carrying casks of rum and pirates drinking ale.

But running away,
What will happen to me?
I have decided, I will stay,
Home is where I like to be.

Brigit Belden (13)
Longhill High School

A Poem Of Poppies

In the fields the poppies grow,
Row upon row they flow.
They are ruby red with long green stalks,
And over them fly great big hawks.
My friend and I went there yesterday,
But we only stayed for a little play.
Hopefully next year there will be more,
Oh what a wonderful ruby galore!

Katie Stevens (12)
Longhill High School

Life

At school,
On Monday just like any other day.
At break,
School is boring in every single way.
It's raining,
There's water everywhere.
I'm wet,
It's so cold, it really isn't fair.
I'm ill,
In bed and I have a lot of sorrow.
I'm dead,
The funeral is tomorrow.
I'm a ghost,
In the afterlife get ready to face my wrath.
I scare,
People that are near and I laugh.

Elouise Date (14)
Longhill High School

Little Hunter

He sees it in the bright blue sky,
Flying above the treetops high.

Oh no! It's gone, it's flown away,
He'll have to find it later in the day.

High in the sky he spots it,
Moves slightly to the left a bit.

Slowly and silently it creeps,
Gets low to the ground and leaps . . .

On a butterfly.

Annabelle Lee (12)
Longhill High School

Lost

The darkness had already swirled out of control
Without me being able to stop it
Covering up the thoughts I was thinking
And
Erasing the memories I longed to have
My mind was endlessly calling for it
To stop
But nothing was happening
My mind was being cleared, it was unstoppable
It felt as if a tornado had hit me
Sending everything in all directions
Nothing I could do could
End this
But what I didn't realise
Was that the nightmare had just
Begun!

Vicky Clarkson (12)
Longhill High School

Speed Sunday

Wind through your hair, burning rubber everywhere,
Speeding on a motorway at ninety miles per hour.
Up, up going up flying in an aeroplane above the seas,
Speeding onto England.
Clink clank speeding on a train now, can't stop,
Let's go on the way home now.
Racing on a path, speeding on my bike won't stop,
Can't now I'm going home soon.
Running to my house, coming to my front door, drop my bike
Run inside, sit down, speed Sunday.

James Foot (12)
Longhill High School

Whose Coat Is It?

The family of tigers were born wild and free,
In a jungle far away from you and me.
They lived in peace, all undisturbed,
'Til a poacher's shot they heard.

The tiger cubs held in gentle jaws,
Are laid lovingly on a cave's hidden floor.
They whimper and whine,
But there is not time,
To lick goodbye.

The brave tigers bolt for distant green cover,
The guns boom out, and their life is over
The snuggling cubs stay quiet . . . in fear,
Terrifying roars of pain, is all they hear.

The parents never did return again,
The fashionable lady never need explain,
Why she simply must have that tiger's fleece,
Please - let animals live in peace.

Tyler Goatcher (11)
Longhill High School

My Tortoise

I have a little tortoise, he lives inside his shell.
He is the size of half a walnut, but has a home as well.
He is a greedy little boy and always wants to eat
Tomatoes, lettuces, kiwi fruit or any tasty treat.
He likes me to stroke him and tickle under his chin,
But when he has had enough of that he pops his head back in.
Arnie is what my little pet is called
He hasn't any hair therefore is quite bald.
Although he doesn't play as such,
Arnie I love you very much.

Ruby Mitchell (12)
Longhill High School

Battle For The Cup

They join in the middle,
They connect
It is a fearsome battle,
Who will win?

After all there has to be a winner,
Who will be celebrating over dinner?
Before that they have to fight
With all their strength and might.

Will it be me?
Or will it be him?
Will I have to flee?
It might go either way,
Time will tell just wait and see.

The battle begins,
Run, run for your life
The world spins,
Will I survive this strife?

Mud flying everywhere,
Bodies dropping to the ground
Friends suffer agony and swear
Will the winning try ever be found?

Pushing, kicking, screaming out,
Connecting, passing.
To me I shout!
'Run, run for my life.'

The war is over,
Fear has gone,
The victory's ours,
Celebrations begun.

I will be celebrating over dinner.

James Yates (11)
Longhill High School

Light

Light! Light! Burning bright, in the darkness of the night,
The flickering flame of a glowing candle,
Sparkling from the iced birthday cake,
Or escaping through the eyes of a pumpkin,
As the pumpkin stares out into the empty space.

Light! Light! Burning bright, in the darkness of the night,
Cutting through the triangular prism,
The colours of the rainbow catching your eyes,
Stealing your attention like a dog and its bone,
Nothing to stop you, as it draws in your vision.

Light! Light! Burning bright, in the darkness of the night,
Look up at the sky, the man in the moon,
Sharing his light to you and the world,
Night after night, just him all alone,
Pleasing so many people with a glorious sight.

Light! Light! Burning bright, in the darkness of the night,
Waiting at the station with the rain pouring down,
In the thick foggy mist, waiting, waiting,
And suddenly out of nowhere come the lights of the train,
The blinding circles gliding nearer and nearer.

Light! Light! Burning bright, in the darkness of the night,
The best of them all in the month of December,
Spinning around a colourful tree,
All mixed up with baubles and tinsel,
What else can it be but the Christmas tree lights?
Light! Light! Burning bright, in the darkness of the night.

Cara Richardson (14)
Longhill High School

I Like That Stuff

Football I like that stuff
Basketball I like that stuff
Fishing I like that stuff
Reading I like that stuff.

Thomas Simpson (11)
Longhill High School

Me And My Brother

I once was small
Then grew gradually
I had a twin brother
Who looked just like me

We were always different
We stood out in the crowd
I don't know why
We weren't even loud

Me and my brother
We couldn't shed tears
We didn't have eyes
We didn't have ears

People started at the bottom of us
Then rose to the top
Little did they know
That we would drop

When this day came
It was a day of sadness
How could one person
Inflict such badness

When we were hit
We came bumbling down
Our parts everywhere
All over the town

Now me and my brother
Rest peacefully in Heaven
Because the day I'm talking about
Is September the 11th.

Victor Laidler (14)
Longhill High School

Sweets I Like

Sweets, sweets, one of the nicest things in the world!
When you eat them they do all kinds of things,
Eat them to enjoy their taste,
Eat them for pleasure,
They are the best treat!
Sweets, sweets, one of the nicest things in the world!

I like sweets.

Lots of people like sweets, but some don't.
It's those grown-ups, who don't,
Keen children are, but the adults are the opposite!
Eat for enjoyment children say!

I like sweets.

Like them and then pass on to others,
Others will learn,
Value them and others will see,
Eager people do so!

Eat them as if they were little bits of Heaven.
My idea is that anyone who doesn't eat them can eat beans!

Zeshaan Zaidi (13)
Longhill High School

Friends

F orever we will always be
R oaming about careless and free
I   want this to carry on
E verlasting love so strong
N ever stopping till the end
D ays so great with you my friend
S taying together is how it should be.
My friends mean the world to me.

Danielle Hilton (15)
Longhill High School

A Dream

As your time draws near
You realise you lived in fear
Fear of the unknown and what might be
What the scientists tell you on the radio and TV.

Everyday thousands are born and die
But at both events people cry
The emotion we show affects everyone
Just like our actions and the things we have done.

The cycle of life is never-ending
Turning, winding and always bending
You can end life as well as begin it
All it takes is a few seconds or maybe a minute.

In the end we are all the same
We have felt the good and the pain
Many things our eyes have seen
They come rushing back as if life were a dream.

Karl Stepney (13)
Longhill High School

Christmas Thoughts

Christmas, Santa, sleigh, snow
Play, fun, friend, foe
Hate, fight, cry, sad
Happy, glad, good, bad,
Naughty, nice, cheerful, kind
Polite, proper, thoughtful mind
Body, soul, spirit, ghost
Scary, Hallowe'en, party host
Gathering, Christmas, sleigh, snow
Play, fun, friend, foe!

Lucy Davies (14)
Longhill High School

London

London, Queen, tubes, Big Ben,
Shops, Harrods, London Eye, River Thames

Cars, coaches, buses, trains,
Taxis, trams, limos, planes

Drugs, racism, Metro Police, crime,
Pollution, crowds, fumes, no time

Happy, amazed, privileged, important,
Tired, crowded, paranoid, impatient

Arsenal, West Ham, Chelsea, football,
Tennis, Wimbledon, hockey, basketball

London, Queen, tubes, Big Ben
Shops, Harrods, London Eye, River Thames.

Emma Gillam (15)
Longhill High School

Nonsense

Hamsters, rabbits, cats, dogs
Lizards, snakes, turtles, frogs
Scared, frightened, upset, sad
Cheerful, happy, mad, glad
Smile, frown, silly faces
Toes, nose, mouth braces
Chain, necklace, bracelet, ring
Prince, princess, queen, king
Families, big, medium, small
Teenagers, toddlers, babies crawl
Excited pets, cats, dogs
Lizards, snakes, turtles, frogs.

Grace Baddiley (14)
Longhill High School

Twenty Years On

Twenty years on
I stand alone.
Looking at the broken city
That once was my home.

Grand sights I welcomed once
Are nothing more than shells.
And people I once held so close
Are simply images of those who fell.

Friends and family;
They long ago left.
And all workers are in prison
For petty theft.

If this is how it is now,
What in times to come?
If this is what has happened already,
What awaits twenty years on?

Courtney Darby (14)
Longhill High School

Untitled

In a land far away where the sun shone and the sky was blue
Under the blossom tree the pretty birds sang sweetly
Everything was how it should be
But along came change and wiped it away
A perfect picture disappeared,
No more sun or blossom tree
The land dark and gloomy,
Everything must change
Even beauty never back again, gone.

Arla Kayne (14)
Longhill High School

The Wonderful Sight Of Wimbledon

The play starts at noon
The courts are getting crowded
The strawberries and cream are ready
The stars are getting nervous
The wonderful sight of Wimbledon.

The sounds of the umpires
The calls of the linesmen
The big names appear
Davenport, Asagoe and the Williams sisters'
They all come to entertain and win
The wonderful sight of Wimbledon.

The centre court has opened its doors
To an unheard of, unseeded newcomer
The crowd goes wild, the champion looks glum
The match is alight and match point is set
The wonderful sight of Wimbledon.

The semi-finals are here
The quiet anticipation of the final looms
The balls crash against the strings, honour and
                                    financial gain at stake
The crowd 'Oooh' and 'Aaah!'
The wonderful sight of Wimbledon.

The last Saturday dawns
The sun disappears - is replaced by rain
The umbrellas are out again
Oh! Cliff Richard entertains
When will the players come out and play?
The crowd is silent.

The covers are off, balls are hit
Cheers, tears and the lifted trophy,
The wonderful sight of Wimbledon!

Ben Taylor (14)
Longhill High School

Fruit Basket

Apples are round, shiny and red,
You can get green ones;
If you like them instead.
The skin is sour,
The inside's sweet,
The core is hard,
That's the part you don't eat.

Oranges are orange, like their name,
They grow on trees,
Like apples, it's the same.
There's smaller oranges,
Called tangerines,
There's other names,
But not often seen.

Bananas are slim, they have a peel,
The skin you can't eat,
Because it's not real.
It's yellow and shaped
Like a crescent moon,
They'll look green,
If you pick them too soon.

Grapes are green, oval and small,
They're all bunched up,
Like bags of marbles.
They grow on vines,
Which are very long,
But because they're so sweet,
They'll soon be gone, gone, gone.

Tonie Lam (13)
Longhill High School

These Big Animals

Running to catch their prey,
These fierce, big animals.
But they're getting extinct,
These big animals.
One by one, animal by animal,
These big animals.
They look so cute, but only some are,
These big animals.
These big ones are not cute,
These big animals.
Tearing things apart,
Not my cup of tea.
These are so big and fierce I don't like them.
These big animals.

Alice Cloud (13)
Longhill High School

Blank Paper

A pencil on the table,
A ruler on the chair,
But inspiration fails me,
So my sketch-pad still stands bare.

I have journeyed through the Amazon,
And swam through many seas,
I have trekked through the Sahara,
But it is still a mystery.

I have so many dreams and plans,
Rolling in my head,
But each one does not seem to fit,
I'll read some more instead.

Lily Robertson (13)
Longhill High School

Scooby

One hot day at a boot sale
I saw a pup without a tail
Ever since then I've wanted a dog
Everyone said I would prefer a mog
'No!' I said
'I want a dog to tuck into bed,'
I nagged my dad for years
One day he was all ears
We got a pup on a foggy night
He was full with tears and fright
But after a while he was fine
He was Scooby!
He was mine!

Joanna Osborne (12)
Longhill High School

Horses

Horses galloping through the grass,
Their manes are swishing really fast.
Horses walking, cooling down,
Then picking up speed to keep going round.
Horses go all day long,
As fast as possible staying strong.
Horses then go to sleep at night,
Can sometimes wake up with a fright.
Horses get used to the bright sunshine,
They then start playing like it's fun-time.
Horses have the rest of the day off,
They eat too much hay and get a bad cough.
Horses sleep throughout the day,
Still keeping a watchful eye on the hay!

Shelley Hunt (12)
Longhill High School

Death Song

My prey I stalk,
In the forest I walk.
The animals are nothing to me,
You will soon see,
The power of me.

Above the river I fly,
Smooth as a human's lie.
The commandments I break,
As life do I take?
You will soon see,
The power of me.

On the ground I lie,
As the birds above fly.
Death is my friend,
As venom I send,
Through veins of my prey,
As they turn to dismay.
You will soon see,
The power of me.

My prey I stalk,
In the forest I walk.
The commandments I break,
As life do I take?
You will soon see,
The power of me.

Michael Overlaet (13)
Longhill High School

My Family

My brother is funny
My brother is mean
My brother is a tennis buff
My brother is slender as a bean!

My baby sister is sweet
My baby sister is kind
My baby sister never cheats
My baby sister is a lucky find!

My older sister is rather smart
My older sister is rather pretty
My older sister has a kind heart
My older sister is very witty!

My mother is a great cook
My mother is a great nurse
My mother loves a really good book
My mother luckily has a full purse!

My dad is a great man
My dad is supportive and kind
My dad helps develop our life plan
My dad is as good as you'll find!

My family has plenty of ups
My family has plenty of downs
Sometimes we all disagree
We don't always live in harmony
But basically our unit is as strong as can be!

Nick Taylor (14)
Longhill High School

All Dried Up

It's still flat, and I'm getting fat
So I think I'll write a poem.
It's to Mother Nature and King Neptune,
Do you know them?

Oh, King, Mr Neptune, deep in your aquatic throne,
Mother, with your consistently unpredictable nature,
You know we can never be at home,
Lest we become engulfed in your turbulent waters.

Oh please have pity on us poor beached creatures.
If I can't surf and feel the wetness so free,
I might as well be eaten by sharks.

Please send us miserable souls a swell or two,
Otherwise this poem is just the beginning,
Of what a dried out surfer will do.

James Hart (12)
Longhill High School

Muffin

When I am lonely or sad
I call for Muffin
He sits in my hands and listens to my problems.
If I ever need a friend
Muffin is there
And he will play with me.
When I need an opinion
I ask Muffin
And he tells me.
I sometimes feel that there is only me and Muffin in the world
And we think up marvellous adventures together.
One day, Muffin's day will come
So we will enjoy his life while we can.

Jordan Green (11)
Longhill High School

The Moon Wolf

The night was silent,
In the wood,
As quiet as the midnight should,
But under the ginormous fir,
A hairy creature starts to stir.
It perks its ears towards the sky,
And hears the sound of owls up high.
The creature pounces on a stone,
To then begin the midnight moan.
Soon all the animals hear the sound,
Which trembles rocks upon the ground.
The moon wolf howls the tune again,
To warn them of the deadly crane,
That takes away their treetop homes,
The rumble as the engine drones,
But now to face another day,
And try to survive in a frightening way.
The moon wolf shakes its shaggy head,
Then lopes back home, to go to bed . . .

James Scott (11)
Longhill High School

Tae Kwon Do

T hrust with flat fingertips
A nd a punch near the face
E ager to win the gold

K icking with all my power
W ondering what move to do next
O h I just got hit
N ow I'm in pain

D o I hit him back?
O r do I sit down and cry?

Charlotte Bishop-Williams (12)
Longhill High School

I Will Never

I will never release a single
Be a model on TV
Or be a millionaire
With a butler and a maid.

I'll never make movies
I'll never fly first class
People will never look up to me
Unless I'm six feet tall.

My name will not be known worldwide
My poster won't be on the wall
But maybe that's a good thing.

Fine wine and limos
Caviar and champagne
I'll stick to Coke and pizza
They can keep fame!

Rosie Parsons (13)
Longhill High School

Our Dog

We have a tiny silky haired dog;
Our little friend is spoilt and loved.

This little bundle woofs and barks,
He tries to bite all the post and leave teeth marks.

He drives us mad and makes us laugh;
He is so small but thinks he is so tall.

We all love and share this noisy mutt
What a character he is.

This little dog really belongs to our mum
This little dog's name is Gog.

Paige Burt (11)
Longhill High School

Scary Clowns

Clowns, clowns always give them frowns
When you turn your back at night
They will give you a big fright
The face is big and scary
Some clowns are very hairy
Clown feet are very long
When you walk past they let out a pong
If you see passed a clown's face
You will see a big disgrace
If you think a clown's a friend
You don't want to meet one round the bend
Just remember clowns are not friends
Clowns, clowns, always give them a frown

Don't invite one for a party
They go hyper on one Smartie
They love to climb a pipe
They only eat fruit that's ripe
Sometimes they drink loads of beer
They make a coin come from your ear
Clowns have a red nose
They always do a funny pose
Clowns, clowns always give them a frown.

Andrew Baker (13)
Longhill High School

Monkey Sister

My sister is like a wild monkey
She runs around the house going crazy
When she eats she eats so slowly
And drives my mum around the bend
And she goes to bed and sleeps like a newborn baby
But when she wakes up again she goes crazy!

Sophie Butterstone (11)
Longhill High School

Winter Play

Shorts are not for me today
Strong winds are out to play

The walk to school is very cold
But I'm okay because I'm not that old

Wind whistles a tune in the sky
Brown leaves get thrown up on high

Frosty grass and ground
Now it's our turn to play around

Shall we have a snowball fight?
No, our brown gloves are on too tight

School's over for another day
Let's hurry home tomorrow is Christmas Day

Day into night curl up tight
My bed's so warm I'll dream all night

All those presents under the tree
I'll dream that they are all just for me.

Dominic Hawkes (12)
Longhill High School

The Storm

Waves crashing against the sea wall like a fury of punching.
The angry pebbles being thrown about like baseballs in
a batting cage.
Seaweed swishing and swirling like a furious snake.
The fish going every which way like lost souls.

The sea calms just like a tiger once it has caught its prey.
Pebbles drop as if they are surprised, like when you see a ghost.
The fish stop as if they had just died of fright.
Seaweed is motionless as if it was waiting to pounce.

Silence is golden, the storm has passed, it happened as if the
sea was in a hypnotised trance.

Amy Coulson (12)
Longhill High School

The Undead Curse

The moon is full, the crows are crowing
The ground does shake, the dead now groaning
The hand emerges from the soily grave
Like a monster from a dark, dark cave.
The dead arise from a deep, dark sleep.
They come out of the ground only to eat.
They cover the city, the people scream.
They all pray and hope it's just a bad dream.
The dead move in to seal their fate
Survivors flee through the city gate.
The dead destroy all in their path
This is a matter of which not to laugh.
The helicopter comes to seal the dead.
And return them to their soiled bed.
They flock to return to the graves they belong.
Until the next time they are to be reborn.

Trent Nealgrove (13)
Longhill High School

My Xbox

I love to play my Xbox game
The PS2's just not the same,
I play in a world of fantasy
And sometimes think, is this really me?

I move the characters with skill and flair
Making them run and jump in the air,
With trigger finger and steering thumb
I play and play 'til they're nearly numb.

With gun and sword, axe and knife
My Xbox moves bring them to life,
My mum thinks it's a waste of time
She doesn't understand, the Xbox is mine.

Nick Turner (12)
Longhill High School

The Best Team

Arsenal football club's our name.
We're from Highbury not White Hart Lane.
We're the captain's very, very best,
So come join us, forget the rest.

We play in red, we play in white
We'll give any team a fight
On the pitch we know our stuff
Four-nil again! That's good enough!

To play in England's premier league
You've got to be good for you to succeed
And to go unbeaten, you're a very rare breed,
That's what we did, oh yes indeed.
So remember the year '03/'04
That's why Highbury's going for more!

Charliegh Mears (12)
Longhill High School

Heaven

Can you see me, I am looking down
I am in Heaven not on the ground?

When you sleep I'll be there looking
Down like Mumma Bear.

When it's cold and snowing outside
I will be there right behind.

I think of you every day when I'm up there.
I pray, pray, pray.

Never leave me Daddy!

I miss you Dad!

Jennifer Brown (12)
Longhill High School

Midnight

The pools of rainwater reflect the orange glow of the street lamps,
And as the clouds drift apart, they reveal bright moonlight that
Illuminates the deserted streets below.
An owl hoots in the distance
A cat slinks silently past
The wind whispers through the trees.
The pitter-patter of the tiny, falling raindrops from the brightly,
Starlit skies, which are slowly turning orange,
For dawn is approaching.
The birds begin to sing, morning is upon us
And midnight has gone.

Rosie Inman (12)
Longhill High School

A Poem About My Dog

Winston is my boxer dog
He has a squashed up face,
And when I take him to the park
He loves to run and chase.

When someone knocks my front door,
He growls and barks a lot,
People think he's very brave
But we all know he's not.

But still I love him very much
And everyone knows I do,
But what I love the least of all
Is picking up his poo!

Keely Ann Bitout (11)
Longhill High School

Untitled

She's like a puppet
She has no life
She's not in control
Things are out of hand
She's insignificant
She can't go on

She fell in a hole
She can't get out
She tried and tried
She just gave up
She feels worthless
She won't go on

Time is running out
She just doesn't care
She wants to be noticed
She wants to be loved
But instead she's thrown aside
Unhappy and depressed

She's been noticed
But it's too late
They should have noticed her before
Because now
She's spread her wings
And gone to a magical place
Where she'll be happy for eternity.

Keely Garritty (14)
Longhill High School

Fish

They sway in the water
Like mental drivers on the A23.
They get caught on a line and roasted for dinner
Like the ugly criminals grilled by police
And they squirm until it gets grimmer.

Joe Panther (12)
Longhill High School

All About Dan The Man

There was a man,
His name was Dan,
He ate a plate,
He only had one mate,
That was the lady who lived in a shoe
But she always had a lot to do,
He always eats porridge,
But never went to college,
He was twenty-four,
And did not even have a door,
He was really poor,
He could not even take a local tour,
He had to stand up in front of the judge
So he gave him some fudge,
He had a job at night,
As he was afraid of light,
He slept in a can,
And did not have a tan,
This is Dan,
He lived in a pan.

Georgina Healey (12)
Longhill High School

Manchester United

Man U are the best,
Ronaldo is the coolest,
They can beat all the rest,
Including the smallest.

Man U are the Red Devils,
Arsenal are the Gunners,
When Man U are on the ball,
We know they are the runners.

Daniel Inkpin (11)
Longhill High School

Speed Sunset

As the sun sets so fast
You hear the hooves of a good creature
It gallops bravely on
The creature's mane tosses wild
Never tame was this shaggy beast
Never stops for an apple to eat
It gallops past with its bright eyes shining
Like menacing lights,
With a prance that's so quick
With wings for its feet
You hear the hooves of a horse
As the sun sets so fast.

Rebecca Stabler (14)
Longhill High School

Friends

F is for forgiveness, which you should always have for true friends.
R is for relationship, which you should always treasure forever.
I is for ignorance, which is something you don't need from
   Someone in bad times.
E is for end, which I'm afraid of because I don't want to lose you.
N is for nasty, which a relationship doesn't need between
   Two friends.
D is for dagger, which is what goes through heart when you lose
   A friend.
S is for special friend, which you would look after and make them
   Feel better.

F.r.i.e.n.d.s.

Faye Maskell (14)
Longhill High School

Our Team

Liverpool, Arsenal,
Man U, Newcastle.
We all support diff'rent teams,
If they win, we cheer,
If they lose . . . oh dear!

They may win one match,
They may win a batch.
In their football shorts and shirts,
They often get hurt,
Perhaps hit the dirt.

In the stadium,
That's where it began.
And at the end, if we've won
The feeling of fun,
Has then just begun.

Alex Ford (11)
Longhill High School

The Road

The road, the road, the open road
I ride on the open it's my friend
The road has twists and turns and bends
The road is bad and quiet.

The road means freedom
 R for the roar of a bike.
 O for orange the colour of the helmet
 A for ambition where you go
 D for delight, the souvenirs you collect.

Wade Eason (12)
Longhill High School

Roaring Inferno

The inferno is a preaching lion,
The urge of hunger to burn its prey.
When he is finished the place will be burnt and grey.
The flames are roaring because the beast has gone away,
To find a new opponent, to find new prey.
Finally, the chaos of war, no one was hurt,
It was lucky, like a four-leaf clover.

Ethan Scanlon (11)
Longhill High School

Fearless

When you're down,
And you can't find a frown,
And you're cold, not bold,
Or got no gold.
That stuff don't make you happy.
When you're ill and snuffly.
All you've got to think of is,
Happiness!

Charlotte Worms (11)
Longhill High School

Toast

I love toast.
Toast in the morning.
Toast in the evening.
Toast in my room.
Toast in the kitchen.
I eat toast with butter.
I eat it with Marmite.
I eat it with everything.
I like it.

Aaron Lovell (11)
Longhill High School

Megan

I love my horse
She is called Megan.

She has a bad leg
She likes to be called Meg.

She loves to eat grass
And she is very fast.

But she knows I love her loads.

Fern Spencer (12)
Longhill High School

Best Buds

We first met when we were small,
But years have passed by so now we're tall.
From mini to big we've been pals,
We've been through thick and thin just us gals.
We're buds to the end and that's a fact,
Friends forever and it's not an act.
We've had some cracks in the past,
But our friendship will always last.

Victoria Gill (11)
Longhill High School

Thunder

T reacherous and strong
H owling and mad
U nleashed fury
N othing gets in its way
D evilish and evil
E ats away at everything
R age and madness.

Tom Wilson (11)
Longhill High School

Spider's Around

Spider's around, crawling around
While spoiling the flowers
Laying velvet white towers,
He's in the large garden,
It's an adventure to him,
A scare for you,
A scare for him.

He's in your room
On your bed,
Hiding in the gloom,
Scaring you to death.

He's now in the bath,
A danger to him,
The water's now on,
So don't save him!

Michael Newman (11)
Longhill High School

World War III In My Car!

My mum and dad, my brother and me
All together it is World War III.
This is not a kind affair
For my brother and I do not share.
My mum and I argue a lot,
Even my hamster would lose the plot.
A punch and a kick
A whack and a smack.
'Calm down before you get hurt!'
I hold my breath and count to three and calm down
How will I be until World War IV?

Toxi Doyle (11)
Longhill High School

My Stupid Fat Cat

I once had a furry tabby cat,
But as time pressed on,
You could say he . . .
Put on some weight!
Then I started to call him my stupid fat cat,
But then he did something dreadful
He ate my goldfish!
He swiped at him,
Guzzled him down,
He then burped the alphabet,
And so I wrote this poem:
My stupid fat feline,
Ate my goldfish,
And pooped on my hat,
Stupid fat cat,
I liked that beret,
So he slept outside on the flower bed.

Jake Lawrence (12)
Longhill High School

I Love Hallowe'en

My name's Olivia,
I love it when it comes Hallowe'en!
I like to dress up as a witch or a devil,
As long as my outfit is clean!

When me and my brother go trick or treating,
We have so much fun!
We've got a favourite neighbour too,
Who always gives us a bun!

Lola McCue (11)
Longhill High School

Around The World And Back

Arr, I am a sailor God, I sail the seven seas.
Arr, my name is Captain Todd; we pirates steal gold and tea.

I've climbed the mountains in Romania,
And seen Uluru in Australia.

Tasted raw hot spices in Vindaloo,
And been to the city of Timbuktu.

Arr, I've seen many a shark,
Orange frogs that tend to bark.

The great peaks of Arctic ice,
Or under siege by large red mice.

Arr, we get gold for herbs, tea and spices,
That we have sold for unfair prices.

We do not care for the fee of sorrow, pain and death,
Back in the day like poor Macbeth.

Arr, I am a sailor God, I sail the seven seas.
Arr, my name is Captain Todd; we pirates steal gold and tea.

Rosie Wigmore (12)
Longhill High School

Football's War

Run along the field,
The battle continues,
Foul, foul, like the gun shot piercing,
Shoot the ball, what a goal, all that's the score,
Kick the ball like bombs falling,
Fire burning the armour,
The game ends the best team wins,
The crowd goes wild,
'What a victory' they all shout,
The game is like a war,
Battling for the cup.

Zoe Wilks (11)
Longhill High School

There's This Gang At School

There's this gang at school,
They beat up the geeks
And embarrass the freaks,
They think they're being so cool.

They started on at me today,
Slapping me round the face,
Scolding me red with insolent comments,
It's not gonna happen again.

When I got home I ran through the door,
No one's allowed in my room,
I let go of my bag and dropped to the floor,
I'm starting with the press-ups.

I'm learning to defend myself,
I'm gathering all my strength,
I lift my rucksack off the shelf,
It's not gonna happen again.

I wait for sleep to overcome the house,
I'm leaving late tonight,
I push open my door and I know they won't rouse,
I'm going to give the gang a fright.

Jess Thompson (12)
Longhill High School

The Albion

Albion win! Albion lose!
Albion score! Albion cruise!
Albion! Albion!
Albion want Falmer
Albion want goals
Albion want Rooney
Albion want Scholes.

Cameron Martin (13)
Longhill High School

Derbyshire

The dry grey stone walls run along the fields,
Sheep lying behind them,
The horses could jump them, but won't,
Cows grazing beside them.

Streams trickling by,
Waterfalls crashing, splashing down,
The spray, you can feel against your face,
So fresh standing by it.

The cliffs stood still and tall, like a tower,
Nothing will pull them down,
Orange and grey the colours of the stone,
Plants grow between them.

Mondays in Bakewell, market day,
Summer in Tissington, the well dressing.
Shops in Buxton, the most well-known place,
All cramped in Over Haddon, except for the spacious fields.

It's beautiful in Derbyshire,
What a lovely place to live,
One day I will be there, I know.

Rachel Raynor (13)
Longhill High School

My Poem

Most of the time my home's a war,
Me and my brother always fighting,
Before even getting into the door,
I'm sure it's against the law.
We try to stop but it goes on more and more.

My brother and I are at war.
Shouting and screaming is a bore
So now he kicks and punches and just asks for more,
We fight and fight our hands turn into claws.
As one wins and the other is on the floor!

Lauren Mutimer (11)
Longhill High School

Cheesecake!

Cheesecake
What more do you need?
Cheese and cake
Are nice indeed
But when together
It's rather wrong
'Cause in a cake
Cheese doesn't belong

Cheesecake
Is thought a treat
But why would you do that?
'Cause cheese isn't sweet
Cheese and cake
Just do not go
What is the point?
I'll never know

Cheesecake
I'm not gonna lie
The thing is
I've never really tried
To eat a slice
It's just too odd
How can you put it in your mouth?
Oh my God!

And that's the end
Of my cheesecake poem
The things I've said
Are well worth knowing
But why people eat it
I'll never know
'Cause the thing is
Cheese and cake just don't go!

Kat Walker (12)
Longhill High School

Alone

Billy! Billy! It's time for your tea!
The voices ring in his head, patronising.
He sits cold in his damp, padded cell.
Alone.
He sits silently shivering.
A danger to himself.
He wouldn't hurt a fly.
Cold sweat soaking him.
Day after day, silent pain.
Slowly devouring his soul.
Day after day, staring at the sky.
He had a family once.
A wife and three kids.
They abandoned him.
Lost in an empty room.
Alone.
Cold sweat dripping from his back.
Silent pain.
Red, restless eyes.
'How are you?'
Patronising voices.
He searched for words.
They had abandoned him.
Silent words.
Alone.

Elliot Hurst (13)
Longhill High School

Feelings

People can be happy, people can also cry.
People's lives are busy as the days go by.
People can be outgoing and people can be shy.
People can have a happy life if they really try.
The art to life is having *fun!*

Lewis Warren (11)
Longhill High School

Basketball Game

As I run down the court, I get ready to shoot,
Standing in the key, eyes on the hoop,
I position my hands for the aim and knees for spring
But I shout as the ball bounces off the rim
Now the other team are sprinting to our hoop,
So I jump up to protect the net, but they score!
It's not over yet!

But the clock is quick
So soon, the match is almost over, nearly out of time,
My friend's got the ball, so I run to the line,
He dribbles and delivers me a pass,
This is our last chance; I've got to be fast,
I really want to win!
I shoot, I score, it's good cos it's six-four!

Connor McLeod (12)
Longhill High School

She

All she could think about
Was the world of cold and fear
No one noticed
No one cared
For she was never seen again
'Did she run away?' they say
Did she disappear?
Did she fly into the sky?
Drop off the end of the pier?
No one really knew the story
The police had no idea
About the girl who disappeared
From this world of cold and fear.

Samantha Sloper (13)
Longhill High School

The Nature Around Us

The blowing trees,
The moving wildlife and the happy,
Little monkey swinging on the branches,

The quick cheetah moving for its prey,
The cold polar bear preparing for the summer.

Flowers blooming as the sun comes out.
Summer's here and everything's happening.

The grass is green and the trees are great,
The owls have gone and there's nothing but birds.

The Downs is shining with its beautiful fields,
The wildlife that is there is happy and jolly.

The rainforests in the world have stopped their rain,
The sun is out and the rain is dying.

The fields are spectacular and they're here to stay,
The birds are coming back from their long trip.

A new day begins and the sun appears again
Why can't it stay like this?
All beautiful and green.

William Keave (12)
Longhill High School

The Station

The hundreds of people lining the platform,
Eating and drinking and chewing on popcorn.
The ground shakes as the train just passes,
Puffing out steam and bending the grasses.

Level crossings and billowing steam,
Clanky signals and coaches that gleam.
The dusty station has a woebegone look,
But as the train passed the platform shook!

Finn Belden (12)
Longhill High School

Brighton Roolz!

I love Brighton, it's so great
Loads of shopping with my mates!
Jewellery, knickers, clothes and more
Churchill Square opens the door!

Pineapple, Mark One, Gap and Pilot
With none of these, the place would be silent.

My favourite shop has gotta be Tammy
Whatever you do don't take your granny!

Check out Athena,
HMV too,
I know this stuff's gonna benefit you!

Out of the Square down to the pier
Get your go-Kart into gear.

Get on that slide,
Get out those ten p's,
As you zoom down don't forget to scream
Wheee!

Candyfloss, junk food sweets and more,
On the pier is never a bore.

You can't beat crazy mouse or that spinny thing
Up in the air it feels like wind.

So don't take the word from me,
Get down to Brighton for a shopping spree!

Annie Bradley (12)
Longhill High School

Life

L iving together careless and free,
I s how I want my life to be,
F riends are important especially to me
E verlasting love is always the key.

Amy Bigwood (14)
Longhill High School

The Fisherman And The Fish

I was lurking in the misty depths of the silent lake,
Pecking at the little specks of food,
I knew he would come and I knew I could be ready,

I crawled up in my car making as little noise as possible,
Softly springing from foot to foot,
Slowly and carefully unfastening my rod,
Creeping nearer and nearer to the lake.

Suddenly the blurred black shape appeared, towering above me,
The shape seemed to shimmer,
Immediately my senses flung into me like a gun bullet.

All at once I saw him and he saw me,
He fled all at once, disappearing from sight,
I wheeled back and let my line flow.

I had to keep near to cover,
Never must I even think of food,
He most certainly is using different food than last time.

Frustration sweeping over my face,
I started to reel in yet another morsel of a fish,
My last cast of the day was out,
Immediately I felt a huge tug on my rod.

I felt something digging into my back,
Slowly I was dragged backwards with a tremendous amount of force,
My eyes full of terror.

I was just about to lift him out of the water with my net,
My heart thudding fast,
My mind only on my rod and net staring wide mouthed.

The pain shooting through my body every limb shaking,
Suddenly my fin ripped,
Relief spreading everywhere.

My line slacked and I just stood there.

Henry Barden (12)
Longhill High School

The War

We sat there in the trench,
We were waiting,
Waiting for the big moment,
Any moment now it would come.

Men were stranded in sewer-like trenches,
Sitting there like ducks,
Debating the near future,
Would they or would they not survive?

We were deafened by guns,
Shooting wildly,
The ground would shake as shells exploded,
Trying to defeat us Brits.

Men were attacking their foes ferociously,
Defending their life,
And their livelihood,
Surely the enemy would fall.

We could see men falling,
Wherever we looked,
Every time we saw one fall,
We would fight back doubly as hard.

Trenches snaked the barren country,
Hiding the soldiers,
They winded until they met the battle,
And there they would stop.

It was time to do it,
We would charge,
Into no-man's-land,
We charged into death . . . the First World War.

Chris Rosier (13)
Longhill High School

The Gun

The gun,
A wicked weapon,
It brought pain,
Sorrow,
Anger.
The bullet comes,
Grinding down the channel,
Breaking loose and curving through the stillness,
Carving a path through air,
And killing.
Blasting a ragged hole,
Shrapnel flying,
A life lost.

It brought pain,
Sorrow,
Anger.
It also brought peace,
Freedom,
Happiness.
A person dies,
But a country rises,
Rejoice,
Unite.
Maybe it's not so bad.

Maybe.

Ben Milne (13)
Longhill High School

My Dog

One puppy with blue eyes
Sweet and lovely
Black and white
He's deaf
But I love him even more
My dog called Buster.

Sean Finucane (12)
Longhill High School

A White Dream

A shimmering blanket lay delicately on the tree,
Its leaves appearing as snowdrops.
Silence surrounded their movements,
The garden's water feature looked pearlescent.

Birds sang to the beat of the falling snow,
Swimming within the overlapping layers,
A cat surveyed its prey,
Waiting for dinner to come.

White, mesmerizing clouds
Waved by in the wind,
A blank canvas lying below.

The snow cascaded down like a waterfall,
Down into a never-ending white dream.

Hollie Groucutt (14)
Longhill High School

Summer

Summer is here at last,
Today the sun is very bright,
Shining high with all its might.

Summer is here at last,
Children playing in the park,
While the dogs run and bark.

Summer it is here at last,
Children splashing in the sea,
Staying 'til it's time for tea.

Summer is here at last,
Pretty flowers coming out,
Buzzy bees buzzing about.

Summer is here at last,
And guess what has just happened?

It's raining!

Melis Topcam (12)
Longhill High School

Hallowe'en

I love it at Hallowe'en, when the stars are in the sky,
And the full moon is at its brightest,
Where all the dark bats fly.

The children visit houses,
With a bag for collecting sweets,
And say, 'Trick or treat!' to anyone they meet.

Watch out for ghosts and ghouls,
And scary vampire bats,
And witches, wizards, dragons,
And big, black cats.

And on Hallowe'en on All Hallow's Eve,
All the little children have tricks up their sleeve,
So that when they visit houses,
And the people won't give them treats,
They scare them with a prank,
And are cross for getting no sweets!

Rose Dutton (11)
Longhill High School

The Bully

Laughing, crying and tears of pain,
He gets up and walks down the little lane,
Wiping his eyes with his torn shirt,
And clearing the marks where he laid in the dirt,
His thoughts inside; *how was he going to survive?*
How was he going to survive?

He turned around and looked at the school
Where he met the bully, the selfish fool
And he said to himself with pride
'He's just a bully he can't hurt me!'
But he knew what he said didn't make a difference
He was coming for him if he liked it or not!

Charlotte Catt (13)
Longhill High School

The Living Present

Standing alone in the field down the road,
The forgotten birthday present stands,
A pony in a silent, forgotten mode,
He thinks of lush fields, they're like different lands.

He was bought for a child by a mother,
Pony was everything for about a week,
Then she got bored, her attention turned to another,
And pony was left, what a cheek!

His fur's full of mud and mats,
He hasn't been fed,
He used to have lots of hugs and pats,
Pony feels as if he might as well be dead.

Then one day he sees a horsebox,
Kind people come and say it's OK,
They lead him over the mud and rocks,
They say that he'll see a better day.

Now pony's at the horse rescue,
In a paddock with a pony friend,
Now he's as happy as me and you,
He knows his happiness will never end.

Don't make an animal feel like he did
Buy sweets and toys for your kid.

Kate Goodwin (12)
Longhill High School

Time

With every dying second, someone else will die,
With every passing minute life will pass you by,
With every laughing hour someone else will cry,
And with every normal day all you ask is why.

Hannah Mitten (14)
Longhill High School

My Heart-Stopper Girl

She was petite and ever so fragile,
She looked so innocent and smart,
But push her with the slightest touch,
And she'd go off and could easily hit the heart.

She would only ever wear black,
Covered in it from head to toe,
But sometimes when light hit her body,
She'd shine and her dull black would nearly glow.

There was no scratch on her in sight,
And she always felt smooth,
However she was always hard - solid stiff,
Like she had something to prove.

She could hide easily,
So people were fooled and unaware,
Never seen until needed,
And you knew she'd always be right there.

Whenever I needed her assistance,
She'd come fast and quick,
People's eyes fixed on her,
Like she was some kind of trick.

Maybe she looked too innocent and harmless,
Maybe they thought it was all a big joke,
But it wasn't and I pulled her,
A tremendous band then nothing was spoke!

I'd peer at the lifeless person lying there,
Thinking this innocent elegant looking girl has done it again,
Maybe tomorrow she'd strike once more
But for the person lying there tomorrow never came!

You see now this girl of mine doesn't seem so fun,
Because this girl of mine is no girl - she's my gun!

Jessica Harman (13)
Longhill High School

A British Rose In German Soil

I watched her kneel in her cell,
Her nurses cap askew.
In dismay, I found myself say,
'Is there anything I can do?'

She turns to me with a smile,
The essence of God upon her.
'If you would, please, monsieur,
Write a letter to my mother.

Let her know I'm not afraid to die,
I realise now that patriotism is not enough.
I must have no hatred or bitterness towards anyone
It is not only my own people I must love.'

Then they came and took her away,
The flowers wilted and died.
Looking at the woman's empty cell,
I lent back on my post and cried.

They told me that she cried too,
As they wrapped the bandage round her eyes.
As our soldiers raised their guns,
Her soul rose to the skies.

I heard they shot her seven times,
And that she didn't cry a word.
Fell silently to the bloodied floor,
And not a sound was heard.

Such an end for a darling rose,
Set out to save poor souls.
And all she got was a gun and shot.
And buried in a German hole.

Erika-Maye Davies (13)
Longhill High School

The Bully Wins!

I saw the bully prowl around the football field
Hoping she doesn't pick a fight with me!
I try to hide by the bushes like a sloth
Feeling nervous, shaky and scared!

My friend had just come to find me, been worried where I'd been!
I told her, I was keeping my distance from the predator who was
                                             about to pounce on me!
She's getting closer and closer, but I don't know where else to go
Sweat was trickling down my forehead and cheek
I didn't feel safe anymore, I feel all alone
Like the fox when the hounds close in!
Terror is coming from within, from the pores of my skin!

Quicker than a flash the predator has pounced
And I was lying sprawled amongst the prickly grass,
The words fight, fight, fight, drowning in my ears
Darkness all around me!
I wish I'd never been born - maybe I won't wake up
Then all the fear and anxiety will stop!

At last my mum believes me
Understands my fear and pain
The bully has been caught and punished
At last I can breathe again!

But I always look over my shoulder
My life will never be quite the same!
Will that bully ever understand the everlasting pain of
                                             being victimised?

Lauren Taylor (14)
Longhill High School

The Ruler Of The Birds

I am the eagle,
I live on blue sky,
I rule the air regal,
The higher I fly.

I am the sky god,
In all of my might,
The lowers all plod,
Whilst my kin take flight.

I am the master,
The thermals my slave,
I dive and dive faster,
My hunger to stave.

I hear my prey bleating,
Unaware of my selection,
I give my cold greeting,
With no chance or protection.

Though I'm the wind keeper,
It's lonely, no mate,
This wound runs deeper,
This is not my fate.

Then I see her,
The courtship we start,
The wind dance occurs,
The dance from the heart.

The fire in my soul,
Is rekindled again,
Loneliness has no toll,
No one to complain.

David Williams (14)
Longhill High School

Terrorists

They plot, they plan, they scowl,
They hunt, they seize, they prowl
They look upon the blameless life,
To do wrong things to the living,
Many people's families,
Do not have any forgiving.

When they strike you don't stand a chance,
People definitely don't sing and dance,
They look upon the innocent life,
To cause mayhem and destruction,
People think they can do what they like,
But they have to follow instruction.

Police and ambulances are all called,
People of the town are most appalled,
They look upon the faultless life,
To try to get away,
The one thing they don't remember,
They have rules to obey.

Breaking news on the telly,
People's legs go soft like jelly,
They look upon the guiltless life,
To help those in grieving,
People have to stay on top and never stop believing.

Coral Gunn (13)
Longhill High School

Karma

Perfect face? Nice disguise;
You're wearing a mask, covering lies;

Looking down on those you don't know;
You're too high up, they're way too low.

Behind your back, you don't know what they say;
The things you do, you think it's OK.

Is it OK to let people get hurt?
Is it OK to treat them like dirt?

You're not perfect, you're not even close;
Who are you to brag, to boast?

There's plenty more who think it, I'm not the only one;
You have loads of flaws; you thought that you had none.

I'm not trying to hurt you back; I wouldn't sink that low;
This is just a warning, just to let you know.

What goes around comes around;
Won't leave a trace, won't leave a sound.

What you give is what you get;
No forgiveness, no regret.

So remember this, before you're snide;
That you can't run, and you can't hide.

For what you say and what you do;
Will always come straight back to you.

Tanya Mestry (14)
Longhill High School

Books

Books, books everywhere
In the kitchen
Under the stairs
In my room
Under my bed
Sits the best book
I have ever read
Princesses and dragons
Lions and ghouls
Kings and queens
It's the best book of all
Brilliant illustrations
Drawn on every page
I love the part when
The lions get locked in the cage
When I finish reading
I get ready for bed
And have great dreams
About the best book I have read.

Maria Nadded-Hannant (13)
Longhill High School

Flower Of Love

The heart is beautiful, delicate and can easily break like the petals
of a red rose,
And like the stem can sometimes be protected by spikes,
Let the wind catch it and it can be taken into places that it's never
been before,
But a strong wind can pull it apart and it will fall to pieces,
It can be given to anyone as long as they want it but sometimes they
give it back,
Without enough light and water it can die,
All it needs is love.

Charlotte Ingram (14)
Longhill High School

Body Of Salt

Night and day, dark, then light
The worst is the long winter's night
The thunder kicks in, and the rain falls down
In these weathers I'm responsible for many that drown

A whirlpool to the left, a shipwreck to the right
I pray and I hope it will soon be light
The birds hear the crash of the waves and away they flee
Nothing for me to watch, it's hard being the sea

When spring comes at least I'm not alone
People walk by, but talking in a drone
Some people stand at my edge throwing in rocks
Wrapped up warm not even thinking about summer frocks

When will it be summer? It's taking so long
The birds will be back with their high-pitched song
People dipping their feet into my waters
Mothers holding tightly onto the hands of their daughters

Summer is here, the first day of the holiday
Looking my best, glistening in the sun out I lay
People put their swimming costumes on and in they come
Enjoying the cool water even though it makes their feet numb

The days have gone by like lightning, as quick as a flash
When the sun shines down and suddenly the cold wind blows,
away the people dash
Autumn is now here so my job for this year is done
The trees take over and chasing the falling leaves is the children's
new found fun

Winter to spring, to summer, to autumn and then back
From T-shirts and swimwear, to coats and rain mac
No one now cares about what I do and how I feel
I'm just the sea; all I can do is wait for summer to come round
on the season wheel.

Megan Sagar (14)
Longhill High School

September 11th 2001, Another Ordinary Day

John Smith, your average family man,
A caring wife, with two teenage children, living in a very
pleasant house,
A corporate suit needed for his corporate job,
Working in the Twin Towers.

September 11th 2001, another ordinary day,
The early morning rush, the burnt toast, and the hurried goodbyes
to his wife and kids,
He left the house, and strode towards his work,
Unaware of what was to come.

Ten minutes later he arrived, entered the lift, up to the fifty-sixth floor,
The lift arrived - *ding* - the doors slid open, he strolled over to his
desk and settled down for work,
A meeting with his boss at one o'clock, obviously for good work,
And a week long holiday in the Bahamas with his family granted in
five weeks time.

John Smith was working on his computer, when he sensed
something was wrong,
An unusual noise he had never heard before,
Like a low flying plane,
He looked up; it was coming straight at him.

He froze, as still as a statue, there was nothing he could do,
He was not religious but he prayed that this could not happen,
His only thought was his wife and kids; he could almost see them
in front of him,
He cursed to himself, why hadn't he spent more time with them?

John waited for his death to arrive,
He'd never felt anything so bad,
The plane was so close now; he could see the pilot's eyes,
Then everything went black, John Smith had died.

Dan Dungate (13)
Longhill High School

I Like Football

Albion win, Albion lose
Albion draw, Albion cruise
Oh Albion, Albion, Albion
Albion want Falmer
Albion want goals
Albion want a lot of things
Including Paul Scholes
Albion like winning
Albion hate losing
But it's just a game of football
So why all the fighting?
I like football.

Joe Dawson (12)
Longhill High School

The 24th

The
Eve before
Christmas Day I
Couldn't get to sleep I'd
Been waiting since May
I *crept* downstairs, saw the tree, grabbed
A chocolate and it fell on me

I ran upstairs
Got into bed
And found a
Big great lump
On my head!

Naomi Berrio-Allen (12)
Longhill High School

Little Scared

Little scared girl
Your ego has burst
Little scared girl
Could it get any worse?
Little scared girl
Look deep inside
Little scared girl
You need to confide

Little scared boy
You need to belong
Little scared boy
Could you do any wrong?
Little scared boy
The tears that you've cried
Little scared boy
I know you have tried

Little scared people
You don't have to hide
Little scared people
You can fight, you can strive
Little scared people
Be who you are
Little scared people
You're gonna go far.

Dawn Richardson (15)
Longhill High School

New York Skyline

The ups and downs of the New York skyline
The Twin Towers stood amongst its brothers
Like proud kings amongst just ordinary others
Thousands of people inside its glass walls
Little did they know the destruction some evil men would cause

The ups and downs of the New York skyline
Fierce scarlet flames danced around the tower
It was the angry eagles that caused that desperate hour
Screaming innocents trapped in a glass cage
How could those mothers, fathers, daughter, sons be the victims
of terrorist rage?

The ups and downs of the New York skyline
The creaking, shrieking legs could take no more
As levels fell into levels, it was then at which they tore
It started to drown into a cloud of dust
The twins knew they had been defeated by terrorists'
unstoppable lust

The ups and downs of the New York skyline
Now miss two members of their family
Like parents miss their children, who lived before quite happily
Like husbands miss their wives, without a chance to say goodbye
Just memories and dreams to keep their loved ones alive.

Eve Otway (13)
Longhill High School

Favourite Food

Icy ice cream,
All cool and clean.
With strawberry sauce,
That's what I mean.

Chocolate is the best,
It puts sweets to the test.
Even when I share it,
I always want the rest.

Scrumptious tasty pizza,
The girl who served it was called Lisa.
Pepperoni was the topping,
And afterwards we saw her mopping.

All this talk about food,
Has put me in a good mood.
I asked the waiter for some more,
But he was a little bit rude.

Emily Woollacott (11)
Millais School

Bacon

I'm feeling in a food mood
What can I eat?
I deserve a special treat.

The fridge is full of yummy food
What shall I choose?
There it is - fresh, lean bacon.

The bacon sizzling in the grill
Turning crispy, how brill!
Now it's cooked, all tasty and hot
Ready for me to eat the lot.

Abigail Taylor (11)
Millais School

My Favourite Things

The sight of a mountain view,
The smell of my mum's perfume.
The sight of water rushing,
The sound of the wind hushing.
Smell of cookies and cakes baking,
Which my grandma always likes making.
The smell of spaghetti and pasta,
Which saves me from eating faster.
I like stroking doggie's fur,
And hearing Max purr.
Feeling my pet Bobby,
The smell of Ottie the doggy.
I like to cuddle my teddy,
Because he's always ready.
And to put my head on the pillow in the evening,
That's something I've got to believe in.
I like to see my family after being away,
I don't mean just for a day.
And I like to get up early,
So my hair doesn't get curly.
I like to go out playing,
Which goes without saying.
And when you go out running, in the sun,
That's when it might be a little bit more fun.
Laughing is jolly,
So you shouldn't be saying sorry.
My grandma's dogs are furry,
But they wake you up very early.

Kelsie Webber (11)
Millais School

My Favourite Things

Listening to sausages sizzling in a pan,
Feeling the soft, sprinkling of sand.
Eating icing sugar out of the packet,
The feel of a ball bouncing on a tennis racquet.
The warm trickle of gooey honey,
Looking at beaches warm and sunny.
The smell of glorious, sweet summer rain,
The sights you see from inside a train.
Scoffing sweets hour by hour,
Sugary, creamy, chewy and sour.
The sight of homework when it's done and dusted,
Chocolate sponge with chocolate custard.
Looking at some wonderful art,
Eating a gorgeous lemon tart.
I could go on for days and days,
Writing for weeks, page by page.
But now I really must be going,
That is the end of my wonderful poem.

Siân Ward (11)
Millais School

The Eagle's Flight

Soaring down in the valley,
Flying through the eagle's alley,
Sailing up, flying high,
How wonderful it is to fly.
Skimming over the water's edge,
Aiming for that rocky ledge,
Gliding up against the cliff,
I need exercise, my wings are stiff.
I see the sea and the glittering sand,
It's wet and gritty, I won't land,
Swooping up against the sky,
Cutting through the clouds,
Soaring up and drifting away . . . away.

Anna Romanowicz (11)
Millais School

My Favourite Things

The sound of the three o'clock bell,
And bacon's the perfect smell.
I like parrots, spiders and mice,
A velvet coat would suffice.
I like apples, bananas, and berries,
Mum when she's had a couple of sherries.
I love the smell of perfume,
And discovering chocolate in my room.
I like the scent of fried egg,
Hot chocolate down my leg,
And frogs are great, they're so lively,
Don't forget cute and slimy.
Silk is beautiful to touch,
A parrot chatting to a rabbit hutch.
The cat's fine fur, soft as a mop,
Now I've started, I'll never stop.
Bacon's great to taste,
And sizzling sausages on the plate base.
Now I'm exhausted, too much to do,
I could go on forever, so could you.

Ailsa Mercer (11)
Millais School

Animals Of The Night

Animals of the night,
Fear to tread in daylight,
Creeping in the shadows,
Under trees and in the meadows,
The bats, the mice, the foxes and owl,
All nocturnal and out on the prowl,
Living and hunting during the night,
Their only guidance, the moonlight,
Midnight chimes out from a clock,
A hedgehog stirs from under his rock.

Amy Polley (11)
Millais School

My Favourite Things

In summer the rustle and bustle of trees,
Delicate flowers, their petals and leaves.
Cold crispy chocolate just out of the fridge,
The running of water under a bridge.
The glorious sight of yellow sunflowers,
Coming back home after hours and hours.
The summertime smell of a freshly cut lawn,
The song of a nightingale at sunset and dawn.
Classical music so gentle and sweet,
Light creamy pasta, lovely to eat!
Silk so smooth, soft as can be,
The sound of the school bell, only at three!
Hop about frogs that my cats bring in,
Nice tasty hot dogs out of a tin.
Canoeing around on Southwater Lake,
The smell when my mum bakes a cake.

I've got so much more to say,
But I'll save it for some other day!

Elizabeth Mullinger (12)
Millais School

Shopping

Out of all my hobbies I have to boast,
That shopping is the one I like most.
Just looking at all the heavenly shops,
Filled with trousers, skirts and tops.
There are so many things that you can choose,
Not only clothes but millions of shoes.
Dwelling on CDs, jewels and books,
Trying on make-up to improve your looks.
Sparkling earrings of diamond and pearl,
They are my weakness, but hey, I'm a girl!
When I shop and buy all these glamorous things,
I feel like I'm in Heaven, floating on wings.

Sophie McKenzie (11)
Millais School

A Slice Of The Best

Feeling fresh air swiping my cheek,
Seeing the views from a mountain peak,
The smell of Nan's fruitcake drifting towards me,
Gliding down white slopes carried by snow skis,
The comfort of friends on a hard day's work,
And the thrill of our speedboat when it suddenly jerks.
My interesting tortoises Charlie and Billie,
The smell of Mum's cooking which is very filling,
Relaxing fresh air as I walk out of school,
Diving into the Pickering's pool,
Being with family when I'm stressed or upset,
My chinchilla Chilli our cute little pet,
Listening to Meggy lazily sleeping,
And awakes when Dad's alarm clock's beeping.
My last lesson's over, the school bell goes,
I cuddle my teddy and watch the night sky glow.

Jessica Langan (11)
Millais School

My Favourite Things!

Scrumptious strawberry jelly, none of the rest;
Mum's only, that's the best!
Fizzy, ice-cold coke fresh from the freezer;
That's much better than a Bacardi Breezer!
Popping bubble wrap so loud and fun;
The cool calming breeze passing by me as I run!
Lazing on the sofa, watching TV;
Playing with my friends Lizzie and Sophie!
Cute koalas under the sun lazing;
The sunset after seven o'clock, now that's amazing!
Melted, creamy chocolate gloopy and ready to eat;
Poured on ice cream now that's a treat!
The fresh, cold water after a long day at school;
The smell of bread cooking, I want it all!

Ashna Hurynag (12)
Millais School

Food

I love food
You love food
We all love food

Fruit
Meat
Vegetables
Pulses
And cereal too

I love food
You love food
We all love food

For . . .
Breakfast
Lunch
Dinner
Or tea

I love food
You love food
We all love food

On . . .
Park benches
Picnic tables
Sandy beaches

I love food
You love food
We all love food!

Emma Farnes (12)
Millais School

My Favourite Things

These are a few of my favourite things,
Bracelets, necklaces and fashionable rings.
Jazzy music, woodwind and brass,
That odd smell in summer of freshly cut grass.
The bell when it sounds at three o'clock,
That is the sound I like a lot!
Pizza - so tomatoey and cheesy,
Maths work that is especially easy!
Lemon - so refreshing and sour
Horse riding for a whole hour.
Fish 'n' chips, soggy with vinegar, fresh from the shops,
McDonald's, fast food and pork chops.
Toast, fresh from the toaster, dripping with butter,
If you don't like that you're obviously a nutter!
Giggles and laughter, and smiles too,
These are things I like to see people do.
After being inside, all stuffy and bored,
The smell of fresh air is something I adore!
The sweet smell of the lavender bush on a hot summer's day,
The excitement of having my friends round to play!
The lovely smell of bread cooking in the oven,
When people in the corridor aren't pushing and shoving!
A trickle and splash of a waterfall,
Playing with my dog and her ball.
The softest, smoothest, shiny silk,
Cookies and a glass of milk.
Chocolate - a milky, creamy, cocoa delight,
The twinkling lights of the city at night.
The beautiful sunset, dominating the sky,
If you don't like that, I truly don't know why!

Natasha Foote (11)
Millais School

The Egg's Fate

Sitting with my siblings, I wait inside a box,
Then upon its cardboard lid, a gentle figure knocks.

My little brother Eggbert, so little and so sweet,
Was cracked open in a bowl, then with a whisk was beat.

Next to go - the little twins, Eggly and Egglepop,
Who after being taken away, to the floor they dropped.

Not soon after the eldest egg was tried,
(He too was broken, then in a pan was fried).

My little cousin Eggward, sat beside a cooking book,
He and I were put in a pan, ready to be cooked.

After we were placed in cups, not knowing that then,
For the end of our little lives we'd be poked by little bread men.

Stephanie Cave (13)
Millais School

My Favourite Things

The smell of fresh creamy cake,
Whizzing around on my fancy skates.
Waking up on Saturday morning,
Watching my sister eagerly yawning.
Feeling my puppy jump on my bed,
Almost landing on my head.
Going on a hot holiday,
It must be somewhere far away.
Off shopping,
While Mum's mopping.
Back to school,
It's rather cool.
The day ends, the bell rings,
These are just some of my *favourite things!*

Sophie Everett (11)
Millais School

My Favourite Things

I like the feel of crystal white silk,
Cereals in the morning covered with milk.
Sizzling bacon in a greasy pan,
The coke being opened from a can.
Sucking lemon, oh so sour,
The loud bell ringing every hour.
Refreshing water dripping off my hair,
Creamy brown chocolate melting in despair.
Guinea pigs squeak, quiet and sweet,
The waft of flowers, smell it in the breeze.
Bonfires burning in the dead of night,
Seeing my friends laughing, what a wonderful sight.
Waves crashing onto great grey rocks,
Sand on my feet, crumbly and hot.
Feeling guinea pigs, warm and sweet,
Having perfume on me is a wonderful treat.
All my family are lovely and caring,
All my friends are always sharing!

Laura Dudley (12)
Millais School

When Spring Is Here

Spring is lovely,
The air is sweet,
Lambs and chicks with tiny feet.
Little flowers poking through,
Pink and purple, yellow, blue.
In the morning's misty air,
Golden sunlight everywhere.
Pretty blossoms on the trees,
The cosy hum of buzzing bees.
Fluffy rabbits hopping round,
Dewdrops forming on the ground.

Eleanor Martin (12)
Millais School

Teatime

Creamy cakes oozing with jam,
And covered in sauce,
Oh how I wish, I really wish,
That cakes were main course.

Fluffy marshmallows are my favourite snack,
They can fill my tummy 'til it's fit to burst,
On my list of favourite things,
Marshmallows will always come first!

Cabbage, Brussels sprouts and spinach too,
Are all a slimy green.
For my perfect teatime meal,
These things would never be seen!

Mashed potatoes and carrots,
A *disgusting* meal!
If Mum gave me this,
Ill I would feel.

But my mum and dad are really great cooks,
When it's time to eat,
Whatever's for tea, nice or nasty,
It's really hard to beat!

Emily Clement (11)
Millais School

Food!

Oh food,
The lovely sight of it,
Oh food,
How we love to try a bit,
There's tangy, crunchy,
Crispy and munchy,
All different kinds of food.
Sweet, savoury, whatever we can find,
We love to eat chocolate - one of a kind!
Everybody loves food!

Lucy Church (12)
Millais School

My Favourite Things

I love to see my guinea pig
But I would laugh at my dad wearing a wig.

I love to see my mum
But I like food in my tum.

The taste of my grandma's potato pie
Before that I run around and jump up high.

The taste of jam oozing out of cakes
And the smell of bread as it bakes.

I like to use my swing and slide
So I can be like a bird and glide.

I like to ride my pony fast
So I can jump over a log at last.

I like my grandma saying hello to me
And she likes a cup of tea.

My guinea pig squeaking is
Like floorboards creaking.

Olivia Catchpole (11)
Millais School

The Elephant

Long, powerful trunks and legs, fast and strong,
Great ears flapping as it runs along.
Grey, rough skin and tusks curved and white,
Short wavy tail swaying left and right.
Running in a herd in harmony,
Until an evil hunter comes and takes its ivory.
Bleeding to death on the ground,
Barely able to make a sound.
Now the creature is just dead and gone,
Yet the rest of the herd still have to go on.
This beautiful animal, happy and free,
Killed for no reason, just ivory.

Jessica Fleig (12)
Millais School

The Under Sea Band

Under the surface of the deep blue sea,
Where creatures like whales and sharks roam free,
A mysterious world begins to unfold,
Of which no human has ever been told,
Along the rolling dunes of sand,
Fish dance to the music of the under sea band,
While a lobster at the front twangs his guitar,
A pair of eels dance the cha-cha,
The octopus rocks and rolls on his drum,
While the tortoise waiters serve up rum,
A whale starts singing to a very pretty tune,
That got even grandad seahorse up and dancing like a loon,
The dolphins started twisting on the rock that was the stage,
And everybody joined in cos the dance was all the rage,
Some sharks came down and eyed up all the fishes on the floor,
'Til the owner of the disco came and showed them to the door,
Then the band struck up a tune which everybody knew,
So they all swam to the dance floor and danced 'til they were blue,
A very famous seahorse and her partner took the floor,
And everybody cheered and screamed or watched in silent awe,
And finally a starfish sang a solo to make you weep,
Then everybody left the club and went to get some sleep.

Ana-Maria Braddock (11)
Millais School

Fussy About Food

I don't like sprouts,
I don't like peas,
I don't like anything that grows on trees.

Sweets and ice cream,
They're the best,
I don't much care for all the rest.

Cara Burnett (11)
Millais School

I Like Fruit

I like fruit,
Juicy and sweet.
Oranges and apples,
Are all yummy to eat.

Warm apple pie,
Strawberries and cream.
A fruit crumble with custard,
All taste like a dream.

Freshly picked raspberries,
That come from the west.
Grapes are my favourite,
They outclass the rest!

This fruit poem is now ending,
I would just like to say.
Fruit is delicious,
Eat some today!

Emma Wilson (13)
Millais School

Food

Eggs, bacon, sausages and beans,
That put on weight and expand my jeans.

Oranges, onions, freshly baked bread,
I like to think about in my head.

Pizza, burgers, nuggets and chips,
Not long now till they stick to my hips.

Doughnuts, cakes, crisps and sweets,
I could not go without these treats.

All this food will do me no good,
Even though I wish it would.

Siân Webber (11)
Millais School

Fish And Chips

'Out of the door, at last we can be together my love.
Right here, where it all started,
By the sea,
Do you remember my love?
When I first came into the shop,
And I saw you winking at me,
From your hot bed of oil,
Then we were sold,
And doused in salt and vinegar,
The atmosphere outside is fantastic,
The smell's delicious,
The sound's wonderful;
The chatting, the seagulls, the tide,
The best way to spend our last moments together,
Don't cry now my love,
It will only hurt for a second,
Watch out my love
Here comes the brown wooden fork,
Here I go my love,
See you on the inside,
Remember I love you.
Yum-yum! Those fish and chips were lovely!
Hello my love,
Together at last,
For eternity.'

Kymberley Goring (13)
Millais School

Jumping Jelly!

When I eat jelly it makes me go hyperactive!
My belly jumps around and wobbles and wibbles!
As I take another bite my hyperness gets jumping!
And I can't stop this feeling of fidgeting and thumping!

Hannah Gates (11)
Millais School

Why Do They Stare At Me?

When I'm walking in the street,
Oh why do they stare at me?
When I'm at home looking outside,
Oh why do they stare at me?
I tell you, I tell you,
I'm perfectly normal,
I tell you,
They stick their teeth out at me.

When I'm at my friend's door, people look,
Oh why do they stare at me?
When I watch TV
Oh why do they stare at me?
I tell you, I tell you,
I'm just like you,
I tell you,
They glare at me.

I'm in my room looking in the mirror,
Oh why does she stare at me?

Abby Gillett (13)
Millais School

Mars Delight

Mars Delight sits in the vending machine,
Without one bite I'm sure I'll scream.
I fumble in my purse for some money,
I'm going mad I'm sure I look funny.
I rip off the foil to see the beauty,
The mouth-watering chocolate, I know it's a cutie.
Just one bite and I just can't stop,
I eat all I can before I might pop.
I've eaten it all and spent all my money,
But at least I have Mars Delight in my tummy.

Emily Lampard (11)
Millais School

I Love My Food

Butter oozing off freshly toasted crumpets,
Milk poured on crunchy cereal,
Orange squash, squeezed into a glass,
Beans sailing in tomato sauce,
I love my breakfast.

Sandwiches with grated cheese,
Rolls with slices of succulent ham,
French bread with pickled onion,
Chocolate biscuits with creamy caramel,
I love my lunch.

Roast dinner with tender meat,
Pizza with spicy slices of pepperoni,
Pie with healthy vegetables,
Roast potatoes with light brown surfaces,
I love my dinner.

Charlie Hollis (12)
Millais School

Fruit

The banana smiles at me with a big grin
The plum looks at me with bruised eyes
The peach is orange and calls to me
'Stop eating too much pie'

The pear smells like a perfume
The orange looks like a big head
The grapes are too mouth-watering
I don't want to go to bed.

The melon is like a glass of juice
The mango is like a lemon but . . .
I like apple best!

Clare Turner (11)
Millais School

My Favourite Foods

I'm going to tell you about the things I like most,
Excluding all of the veggies and of course the cheese on toast.

I really do like chewing gum, chocolate, sweets and cakes.
But I also love things that most other people hate.

Take gherkins for example, straight from the jar,
Pickled onions, shrimps, prawns,
But cockles are best by far!

I really do like Doritos when they're dipped,
I also love mussels but not green lipped!
I like red grapes and lovely ripe plums,
The juice of which I suck off my thumbs.

To snack on, I eat freshly cooked bagels,
I'll spread on the butter and so I'll be able
To eat what I like, whenever I want,
I got to go now, Mum's made my croissant!

Sarah Rose (12)
Millais School

The Land Of Eternal Darkness

In the land of eternal darkness, where the sky has turned blood-red,
In the land of eternal darkness, the starving are never fed.

In the land of eternal darkness, white light and searing pain,
In the land of eternal darkness, you'll never laugh again.

In the land of eternal darkness, where the birds will never sing,
In the land of eternal darkness, the one-eyed man is king.

Louise Riddles (12)
Millais School

The Last Of The Blackberries

Sweet, succulent blackberries
Black, fat and juicy
Hanging off brambles
Causing child scandals
When they get all stained.

Baking in the oven
All in a pie
Crisp and crunchy
Smells yummy.

Served in a bowl
Sweetened by more sugar
And the berries eaten whole.

Every crumb gone
No more for the eldest son.

The last of the blackberries.

Joanne Marychurch (14)
Millais School

Kitchen

Mum's cooking in the kitchen, what can it be?
I peek round the kitchen door, what can I see?
I see pots, pans and a dirty dish.
I see a crispy, battered, yummy fish.
I see small, slippery, runny beans.
I see it splashed all over Mum's jeans!

Kelly Lord (11)
Millais School

Soul Food

When I take the very first bite,
Of any sweets or choccy,
I'm satisfied deep inside,
I'm dizzy, my vision goes foggy,
It warms me up when I am cold,
It cheers me up when I'm in a mood,
It calms me down when I'm panicking,
Oh what would I do without you soul food?

My mum says I'll get spotty if I eat a lot of choccy,
My dad says I'll get fat if I eat a lot of that,
My mum says it's not good for me,
But I don't really care,
Cos fast food is my goal,
And
Chocolate's good for my soul!

Caitlin Egan (11)
Millais School

Little Banana

'Little banana, little banana
Where have you been?'
'Gathering apple to give to the queen!'

'Little banana, little banana
What did she give you?'
'She gave me a banana as big as my head!'

Sarah Whitehead (11)
Millais School

Simply In My Head

Do bamboo shoots really shoot?
Do runner beans really run?
Do pumpkins really pump?

Or is it just all simply in my head?

Do cucumbers really cue?
Do peas really pee?
Do casserole dishes really roll?

Or is it just all simply in my head?

Are carrots really cars?
Are cupcakes really cups?
Are chocolates really late?

Or is it just all simply in my head?

Is flour really flower?
Is bubblegum really bubbles?
Is seaweed really the sea?

Or is it just all simply in my head?

Are eggplants really eggs on plants?
Are potatoes really pots with toes?
Are pineapples really pines with apples?

Or is it just all simply in my head?

Emily Rex (12)
Millais School

A Chocolate Love Story

Said the Caramel Caress, to the strawberry Kiss,
'Will you come with me to the chocolate box ball?
We will dance all night amongst the hazelnut swirls,
Come with me, I'll give you a whirl!'
The raspberry parfaits will gasp, 'Who are that pair,
The one with the flowing pink dress and him, with the shiny
smooth hair!'

Then said the Strawberry Kiss,
'Would I give it a miss?'
So they went arm in arm off to the chocolate box ball.

The Orange Cream put on a sticky bow tie, he said,
'If I muck this up, I surely will die!
I will wait in my case, for my true love fair,
The one with the pink dress, and flowing hair!'
But she never showed, he sat there and wept,
Runny orange tears, he wept and wept.
Then his friend next door said,
'It was that Caramel Caress who took your true love fair,
The one in the tray below us, with the shiny smooth hair!'

The story ends in a tragic way:
The Orange Cream was plucked from his bed that day.
He stuck fast at first, but then was given a pull,
And yes, you've guessed it; he was eaten whole.

Holly Batchelor (13)
Millais School

Ode To A Yoghurt

I am a yoghurt,
Bet you didn't know that.
Full of slushy vitamins,
And three-point-nine grams of fat.

I am a yoghurt,
Sitting boldly on a shelf.
With the cheese nattering beside me
And the butter singing to itself.

'Have you heard the news?'
The egg asks his wife.
'Old Yorick's nearing his sell-by date
He'll soon lose his life.'

My name is Yorick,
Yorick Yoghurt as I'm called,
And I'm just sitting here when Ma'am
Opens the door, and looks at me appalled.

'Oh dear, oh dear, oh dear'
Says the missus to herself,
And she reaches down into my prison,
And plucks me from the shelf.

She will eat me soon, I know,
And I'll behold my wondrous fate,
In a place where yoghurts all play happily,
And there are no sell-by dates.

So goodbye to you mortals,
And, please live a better life,
Than a yoghurt in the freezer,
Sitting next to the bread knife.

Rebecca Tye (12)
Millais School

Food Fight

It's lunchtime
The teacher left the classroom
Let's all celebrate
She's gone to the staff room
Because she's late
Now we're all alone
We can have some fun
We can talk on the phone
And play in the sun
But I have something better that everyone can play
We can have a food fight
Oh, but what will the teacher say?
She will get a fright
But that serves her right

Oliver peeled the orange
Sam squashed the sandwiches
Tom threw the tomatoes
Chris caught the crisps
Ben bit the biscuits
Alex ate the apple
Lucy lobbed the liquorice
Jess jumped on the jelly
Peter popped the popcorn
And oh what a mess!

Now it is so pretty
Food is everywhere
Oh it is a pity
That no one will dare
To go and tell the teacher what's been going on
To go and tell the teacher that something is wrong!

Natasha Knight (13)
Millais School

Banana Split

Start with a banana
Curved like a grin,
Next get the ice cream
And scoop it out the tin!

Two scoops of ice cream
Covered in chocolate sauce,
Sprinkle on the nuts
And you'll need a spoon of course!

Eat up the banana
With the ice cream,
Sticky chocolate sauce and nuts
It tastes just like a dream!

Soon it's all over
I mean all over my face
And Mum says I'm a mucky pup
Cos I always lick my plates!

Victoria Paterson (12)
Millais School

The Feast

Juicy, sizzling spare ribs,
Cooking on the barbeque,
The dark syrupy sauce,
Bubbling and dripping,
All the mouths are watering,
In anticipation of the feast!

Elizabeth Blount (11)
Millais School

The Disgusting Bits

Mushy peas soaked in vinegar,
Brussels sprouts in gravy,
Parsnips with butter,
Olives in jars from Italy,
Burnt shepherd's pie with soggy vegetables,
Seafood in green sauce,
Lamb and veal with roast dinner,
All of the soggy lettuce in a salad,
The brown bruises on chips,
The crust of thick bread,
The skin off jacket potatoes,
The burnt slices of cake,
The walnuts from the icing,
Her home-made custard with bits in,
The cream that went off years ago,
Burnt roast potatoes,
The fat on the ham in the sandwiches,
Cold hot chocolate in unwashed mugs,
Pasta gone cold,
With the sauce that went lumpy,
Home-grown raspberries with bugs in,
All these things my gran forces upon me!

Megan Clark (13)
Millais School

Sometimes

Sometimes,
When I'm neither awake nor asleep,
But somewhere in-between,
I see a place,
A special place,
A place just for me!

In this place there's no anger or hatred,
No wars or injustice,
No sadness or worry.
In this place there are no crimes or punishments,
No one cries, shouts or screams.

In my world everything is perfect,
Everyone is happy, laughing and bright.
In my world everyone feels included,
And everyone's important, whether rich or poor.

Then,
Suddenly,
Those precious seconds are over,
And the world is just as it was yesterday,
And the day before and the day before that.

Isobel Darcy (12)
Millais School

Truth

You think you know me,
But you don't.

You think you know,
My deepest darkest secrets,
But you don't.

You think I have walked this Earth,
For seven thousand years,
Yet I still don't know when I'm being tricked.

Being taken by surprise,
Was a thing of the past.

I see you sneaking up behind me,
Laughing at my tale.

Idle chit-chat no longer excites me,
I have no time for stories,
I have no time to waste.

You know the outer side of me.
But you will never,
Never know the truth.

Laura Bartlett-Short (11)
Millais School

Soldiers

Standing to attention,
In rows along the plate.
Glistening butter armour,
All waiting for their fate.

The first one meets his destiny,
Plunged deep into the yolk.
Now this one's done his duty,
To all the toasty folk!

One by one they're eaten,
Drowned in orange goo.
All of them that is,
Except the last two.

They're hardly ever eaten,
The ones that no one trusts.
Disliked, rejected, set aside,
And just because they're crusts!

Chloe Watson (13)
Millais School

Blue

An indigo starry night,
The clear sky on a sunny day,
The songs of sadness,
Someone in the depths of despair,
Dark nearly black,
But forever blue,
Cold inside your soul,
Calm and cold is everywhere.

Sophie Wright (11)
Northease Manor School

Home Is . . .

Home is . . .
A place to feel safe
Somewhere to relax.

Home is . . .
Shelter under a roof,
Where good company is.

Home is . . .
Peace when you need it,
Having a room with a good bed.

Home is . . .
Watching TV when it's raining.

Home is not home when . . .
You feel in danger,
You feel tense.

Home is not home when . . .
There is not a roof for shelter,
There is no one to be with.

Home is not home when . . .
There is no peace,
There's nowhere to sleep.

Home is not home when . . .
There's no music.

Joshua Moxley-Wyles (15)
Northease Manor School

Yellow

Golden daffodils blowing in the field,
Shining coins freshly made from the bank,
New bananas from the tree,
Yellow custard on my spoon,
The golden sun,
The yellow moon.

Angelo Gelman (11)
Northease Manor School

Home

Home is a safe place where you make wishes,
Filling you with big cuddles and kisses.
Where your loved ones welcome you with open arms,
Protecting you from all the harms.
Although my family does not agree with my faith,
At home I still feel really safe.

You can walk around naked,
And still feel sacred.
You sit at night together eating dinner,
Telling them what your day consists of and how you're a winner.
You get to replay the exciting things you learnt that day,
And how you run and play.

You all sit in the sitting room,
On the telly the news shows us third world gloom.
Fighting over whose got the remote,
You all watch the Americans vote,
The fires beaming upon your faces,
And you all gobble up strawberry laces.

Home is where you have bubble baths at night,
And get told about the wrong and the right.
Where you go to sleep,
Reading books that make you weep.

To wake the next day,
And stick to your way.

Hannah Swan (16)
Northease Manor School

Red

Red poppies swaying in summer fields,
But danger may lurk around the corner,
Blood given for emergencies,
Fire in the Devil's eyes,
Roses on Valentine's Day,
For someone you love.

Henry Noakes (11)
Northease Manor School

Memories

You can forget them
But it will always come back
Worse than ever before
Pushing into your vision
You can't hide the tears anymore.

You can hide them for a while
At least during the day
But at night you remember
You feel so scared and alone
You can't help but cry.

There is a way
You can fight back
Stand up to the thing that scares you
Do not let it beat you.

Angharad Collier (14)
Northease Manor School

A Home

A home should be a happy place,
Where fighting and arguments should not take place,
A home should be a loving place,
When you enter you should be welcomed with a loving embrace.
A home should be a place you love,
Whether you are going through highs or lows,
A home should be a place you love even if you have nowhere to go,
In a home you shouldn't feel like a caged bird, wanting to fly free.
The world is a difficult place without a home.
A home should be built on respect and trust.

Heather Reid (16)
Northease Manor School

Love

You never plan to feel this way,
It creeps up on you when you don't expect.
Can it really be here to stay
Or will I be a reject?
You hope it will stay forever
Never to fade
Always together.
Sitting in the cool shade,
Dreaming of tomorrow with you,
Sat thinking of the way you smile,
Not listening to people go, 'Boo!'
To find you I would run a mile,
Throw all that life can throw at us.
Through the storms and the trouble,
Loving you is all I want.
I would give up everything
Just to spend my life with you,
Never apart,
In my heart forever you will stay.
Can you promise me you feel the same way?
Together we will stay,
Letting the way we feel hold us,
Not caring about others.
Just you and me,
That is the way I want it to be,
Under the stars,
And moonlit lake,
The bird will fly,
But I will not care,
It is just you and I.

Abigail Besley (13)
Northease Manor School

Our Planet

Cold, cold, cold
Dark, dark, dark
Nothing but dark
No light
Black
No life

A point in the darkness
A light
Hope
Life
A new world

Water dripping
Drip, drip, drip
Plants, animals
A new chance

Animals swim in pools, rivers and lakes
Plants can grow free
Birds sing in the trees
Beautiful colour all around
A rainbow

But then black clouds cover the sky
Man has arrived
Blackness looms
Pollution and darkness consumes the world
No *freedom*
The blue planet is no more.

Anna Maycock-Frame (14)
Northease Manor School

Red

Red, red can be nice,
Red, red can be evil,
But it's strawberries I like.
Red soldiers in the war,
Poppies to remember all,
Valentine's is in the air,
Red hearts everywhere.
Red, red can be nice,
Red, red can be evil.

Shannon Elliston (11)
Northease Manor School

Red

Red is . . .
Blood spilt by the Devil,
An angry face,
The fire in a bull's eyes,
Poppies for memory,
Jam on my toast,
A favourite colour in the paintbox,
Red hearts for love.

Jack Roberts (11)
Northease Manor School

Blue

A cold winter's morning breeze whips against you,
Shivering in the Tudor Hall,
Bright blue sea on holiday,
The colour of the sky with fluffy clouds,
Blue is the colour of sadness,
Feeling blue can make you cry,
Fluffy navy school jumpers against you,
Make you feel good.

Ellen Redhouse (11)
Northease Manor School

Skiing

High up the mountain is another world
The world of skiing
Green, blue, red and black

Dressed up warm so you don't freeze
I seemed to take ages to get to the top
Looking at all of the good views
You get there and don't know what way to go

You finally get going and start to warm up
People fast and slow
The wind blowing in your hair
Snow plough or parallel

Snakes of people passing by
People in the distance
Having fun for some
And worry for others

Moguls and jumps
In, out and over
Jumping high
Mind the trees

Not another chairlift
Bruised backs of the legs
It is so slow and cold

Skidding on the ice
As people struggle through the powder further up
Can't see where I am going
I just hit a rock!

Rebecca Bentley (15)
Northease Manor School

What Is A Home?

A home is a place where one feels safe and comforted
A home is a domain where one can get away from the raging storm
A home is a dwelling where one can hide when the world
                                                    is contorted
A home is a state where one can escape the boring norm
A home can be a plateau where many can share warmth and love
A home can be a dark place where dreams are shattered and
                                            nightmares are born.

Lucas Rajpaul (15)
Northease Manor School

Parents' Sayings

'Come to the dinner table now.'
'Do it yourself.'
'Where is your bag?'
'Help me do the washing up.'
'It's time you were in bed.'
'That room is a mess,
Clear it up!'
'Who made that mess in the kitchen?'
'Get up, you'll be late.'

Sophie Blume (12)
Patcham House Special School

In My Dad's Pocket

In my dad's pocket you will probably find . . .
A car key for a greeny-grey car
A sticky crunchy chocolate bar
Some clangy shiny fresh money.

Kelly Gunn (11)
Patcham House Special School

My Brother's Pocket

In my brother's pocket you will probably find . . .
A bloody finger,
Some snotty tissues,
A piece of chewed up pizza
He didn't like and spat out into his pocket,
A few used cotton buds,
A lump of melted chocolate
And a used bloody plaster.

Keifer Hall (11)
Patcham House Special School

Policeman's Pocket

In a police officer's pocket you might find . . .
A pair of handcuffs,
A mini shotgun,
A used bullet,
A confiscated pepper spray,
A Swiss army knife,
A torn photo of a missing person
And a lucky charm to keep him safe on the streets.

David Hall (11)
Patcham House Special School

Parents Sayings

'Clean your bedroom young man.'
'Do your homework or no pocket money.'
'You are late for school.'
'Have you done your washing up?'
'Turn the TV off and get ready.'
'Get out of bed, it's time for school.'

Christopher Hammond (13)
Patcham House Special School

This Is Just To Say

I have taken your donuts and hamburgers
That you bought at the shops yesterday
They looked so delicious
I feel sorry and I am.

Evan Hilton (11)
Patcham House Special School

In My Pocket There Is . . .

In my pocket there are some Yu-Gi-Oh cards, dog-eared,
A box of melted chocolates,
A miniature glasses' case that fits,
My rusty mobile phone,
Some gooey hair gel,
A new and shiny golden one pound piece,
A half bitten cookie,
An unused tissue,
A marked Gameboy Advance SP
And a crumpled agreement form.

Jamie Moore (11)
Patcham House Special School

Not Only . . .

Not only . . .
Did I get all my spellings right
But I also got a sticker.

Not only . . .
Did I have Sam round to my house
But Daniel invited me round to his.

Lawrence Harmer-Strange (11)
Patcham House Special School

Things That Parents Say

'It's time to get up now''
'Go wash your hands.'
'Be polite!'
'That's enough TV for today!'
'Tidy that room now!'
'If you don't hurry up you will be late.'
'Do your homework.'
'You're late again, you're grounded!'
'It's time to do your chores!'
'Maybe you should make some new friends.'
'I am just doing this for your own good!'
'If you don't eat your vegetables you will turn green.'

Bruce Leathead (13)
Patcham House Special School

Parents Always Saying No

'Can you wash my socks?'
'No!'
'Can you get me a T-shirt?'
'No!'
'Can you get me a drink?'
'No!'
'Can you turn the TV on?'
'No!'
'Can you get me a biscuit?'
'No!'
'Can I go to bed?'
'Yes!'

Sarah Steele (12)
Patcham House Special School

Baboon See You Soon

One day in June
A big baboon
Will see you soon
Back on the moon

A small balloon
Flew up too soon
The big baboon's
Back on the moon

Farewell baboon
Who's on the moon
I'll see you soon,
One day in June.

Joseph Cooke (11)
Patcham House Special School

In A Girl's Head

In my head
There is a brain
There are questions to be answered
Like is God real?
Or how much pocket money have I got?
Or will I complete my Zelder game?
And will I grow?
And there is also one more thing
When will I have my turn to be a mum?
And what child will I have?

Leanne Dearling (11)
Patcham House Special School

Break Up, Make Up

I'd like to be your friend,
I'd like to start anew.
I know I've got other friends,
But none quite like you.

I want us to be friends,
What is it I can do?
There has to be at least one thing,
I want you back as a friend, it's true!

I'd like you as a friend,
I know I get kind of stressed.
I know I say you're annoying but,
Really you're the best!

I'd really like to be friends,
I don't care what others say.
To tell you the truth, I've always liked you,
Just give me some space, is that okay?

Charlotte Bothamley (11)
Rydon Community College

The Silent Anhinga

Tranquil as a lake,
Diving down, spearing its prey,
Admiring itself in the bright sunlight.

Cautiously stalking its silent meal,
Peacefully drying off its agile wings,
And as clever as an anaconda coiling its prey.

Sharp-eyed like a falcon and as black as darkness,
As beautiful as a little butterfly,
And diving like an Olympic spear.

William Steer (11)
Rydon Community College

Friday Football

Down in the sports hall,
On a Friday night,
We have a game of football
It's a terrible sight.

The boys kick the ball
From one end to the other,
And one by one they fall
And run to Mother.

They continue the game
Every Friday without fail
And despite all the shame
They play, because they are male.

Michael Harkness (11)
Rydon Community College

The Night

The night is always on time
The night is always with light
The night is always mysterious
The night is always serious
The night will always be there
When the sun falls asleep

The day
The day is something with light
The day will always have a sun
Or clouds
The day will never be dark
The day will never ever let you down
Even when you are at school.

Julia Hartley (11)
Rydon Community College

A Great Nation

The great Uluru
Standing alone
In the vast
Red Sand Desert,
A place of Aboriginal magic.

Every colour imaginable
Is on display at
The Great Barrier Reef
Coral of all shapes and sizes,
Backing onto a beautiful sea.

Heat and humidity
It is all there
In the rainforests
Home of great fir trees,
With their amazing roots.

The non-moving sails
Of the Sydney Opera House
A place of great music
And fabulous acting,
A symbol of this modern land.

You can smell great wines
Everywhere in Rutherglen
A small town it may be
But at every turning,
A grapevine is visible.

A dramatic land
With a spirit of its own
Which speaks to us
Without words,
Behold Australia.

Will Chambers (11)
Rydon Community College

Enchantments

All these spells
And all enchantments,
Gather to dwell
In the name of enchantments.

Witches and wizards
With tangled black hair,
Look like lizards
Who like to glare.

Fairies still scared of trolls
And witches still wearing black,
Pumpkins still baited in bowls
And when you look round, you
Won't
Want
To
Come
Back!

Georgia Pettman (11)
Rydon Community College

Haikus

War
Long, long, long waiting
Load, close, finger on trigger,
Alive? Shot, gone, dead!

Flowers!
Spring will mean flowers.
Blossom, blossom and blossom.
Today, tomorrow.

Chanteé Jansen Van Rensburg (12)
Rydon Community College

Animal Rights

There are animals out there
Who need a brand new home
They have been abandoned
Now they're all alone

There are animals that have been hurt
And been through a terrible pain
That's why they need a new life
To start all over again

Some animals are kept in cages
Which is very unfair
Why don't you let them free,
They don't have another life to spare.

I have a guinea a pig of my own
Who I love to bits
I feed her daily
And I give her a kiss.

Chelsea Snoad (11)
Rydon Community College

Christmas

Hope for reconciliation at home and abroad
Fun for all the children in the world
Togetherness with the family
With no arguments to cause an atmosphere
Have a laugh at no one's expense
Food on the table, enough to satisfy
Warmth for the elderly and the very young
Friends to care
And please Santa remember me.

Joe Fish (12)
Rydon Community College

A Poem About Life

Roses are pink,
Violets are small.
This poem I'm writing
Makes no sense at all.

The cat is fighting
The dog is growling
Everyone's grouchy
The whole place is howling.

My dad is so funny
My mum is so fun
My sister is always screaming
Then so is everyone.

Then Christmas comes along
And everything is fine
First we open presents
Then drink champagne and wine.

My poem is about life
And how it is unfair
There are some wonderful times
But the bad ones beware!

Natalie Bate (11)
Rydon Community College

Vegetarian's Funeral

Snotty noses,
Runny eyes,
The coffin's buried,
But no meat pies.

The church is old,
The people cry,
The day is cold
But no meat pies.

Dan Brennan (11)
Rydon Community College

You Let Me Down

You let me down.
I am going to find your town.
In my dressing gown.
I am going to bring you down.

I am coming.
I'm going to be stunning.
Whilst I am running.
I will also be stunning with the gunning.

Don't forget you owe me that bet.
Don't forget you lost my pet.
Don't forget, pay the vet.

I am going to catch you in my net.
With help from the vet.

You are dead
I am going to shoot you in the head.
I might catch you in bed.
That's what the doctor said.

Joshua Rideout (11)
Rydon Community College

The Game - My First

When you're walking to the ground
For the first time. You feel nervous,
A beam of nerves go down your back.
You sight Stamford Bridge, massive, sitting
In the middle of London with fans shouting
And signing at the top of their voices.
Then you slumber down quietly.
The players burst onto the pitch, the
Crowd go bananas. Zola, Zola scores!
You jump up, amazed and happy
Whilst the away fans sink low. Walking
Out of the ground with a joyful crowd
For winning the match. Well done lads!

William Busby (11)
Rydon Community College

The Concert

On Saturday morning,
The car drove off.
Finally we got to Crawley,
At twelve noon.
The doors don't open till one o'clock,
What are we going to do?
We went to get some popcorn
And coke for a drink.
The doors finally open,
We go in and get our seats
All the fans were yelling,
Yelling 'I want Busted!'
Then . . .
With a flash of lightning,
And a puff of smoke,
Three dark figures,
Came out from nowhere.
Then we saw Busted,
And we all went crazy.

Megan Harber (11)
Rydon Community College

The Kestrel

Stealthy as a 'OO' agent
Haunting its prey
Hovering silently by the motorway
Deadly as a knife it suddenly attacks.

Swallows yelling for help
Cries of horrific pain
Blood splattered everywhere
The killer cries out with joy.

All has gone quiet
Unnoticed in the dark
Sharp eyes darting everywhere
The kestrel is triumphant.

Lewis Yearsley (11)
Rydon Community College

Dark Night

Pitch-black as a raven's wing,
Stars which look like scales off a fin,
The moon shines like a pearl from under the sea,
With the sky as high as twenty skyscrapers,
The night is a wonderful thing.

At night, out of the bushes crawl little beasts,
The owls which spread their wings like hawks,
Badgers which scurry about looking for food,
Foxes creeping through fences to get to chickens,
The little beasts always have fun outside.

When I'm tucked up in bed I hear all sorts of sounds,
The weird creaking sound of the rusty radiator,
The bed shaking on the metal poles,
The racket of dogs howling outside in the night,
But I know I'm still safe.

David McKilligin (11)
Rydon Community College

Late Again Miss Howie!

'Why are you late again Miss Howie?'
'My dog, Bob, died Sir!'
'It died?'
'Yes Sir.'
'But I thought your dog died yesterday?'
'It did Sir.'
'So how many dogs do you have Miss Howie?'
'Twenty-three Sir.'
'Twenty-three?'
'Yes Sir.'
'That's a lot!'
'I know Sir.'
'Wait a minute, isn't that the same number of days till the end of
the year?'

'Um, maybe!'

Becky Howie (11)
Rydon Community College

Homework At The Weekend

Homework at the weekend,
Gets in the way of friends.
I know that I must do it,
But it seems it never ends.

Everybody's in the garden,
And they're all having fun.
But I am doing my homework,
Stuck till I get it done.

I'm trying to write a poem,
But I really cannot think.
Of anything that's interesting,
To write with pen and ink.

The birds are chirping loudly,
The leaves are falling down.
The colours of the garden now,
Are green and gold and brown.

I think of when I'm finished,
And what the class will say.
I hope my teacher likes it,
And I will get an A.

This homework's never-ending,
But now I've found a way.
At last I think I've finished,
And can go off and play.

Imogen Bowen-Davies (11)
Rydon Community College

A River's Life

A stream gets bigger,
All small and loud,
It's like a baby crying at night,
The water shimmers in the light,
As blue as a sapphire,
As blue as the sky.

Soon it flows into a toddler,
The toddler starts to speak,
The stream gets quieter, faster too,
It's like an open air rapid swimming pool.

It flows into a child,
A child so cute and calm,
It sparkles like a diamond,
A girl's best friend,
It bubbles and meanders its way down,
The hill.

It meanders into an adult,
Round hills to make its way to the,
Mouth.
It inspires grass to grow.
It's getting older and stronger,
Its mouth is at the end of the,
Life.

Taome Gardner (12)
Rydon Community College

Knitting

I got changed into my school clothes,
And then went off to school,
My first lesson was knitting,
And my teacher had her hands full of wool.

Teacher said, 'Why are you late?'
I said, 'Honestly Miss, it was not me!'
She said, 'Then who was it?'
I said, 'My form teacher wouldn't let me free.'

Finally the end of school
My finger was in pain
Mum was standing there with wool at the door
Here it goes again.

Knitting can be good
Knitting can be zigzag
Take my word for it
Knitting is for hags.

Charlie Cuppleditch (11)
Rydon Community College

The Golden Bird

He's the king of speed
A swift murderer
With power to rip and tear

The majestic predator
The royal bird
With shining gold-like feathers

Razor talons devastate flesh of prey
Yet lovingly caress young in the nest

He soars high on the wind's waves
Silently 'surfing' thermals with grace

A regal ruler of the sky.

Adam Cheesman (10)
Rydon Community College

TV

TV is such a wonderful thing,
Don't you agree?
It's something to watch,
When making dinner for three.

TV is not a wonderful thing,
Don't you agree?
When your favourite show starts,
You always need a wee.

TV is such a wonderful thing,
Praise the person who invented it.
But whoever made electric toothbrushes,
Was just such a twit.

TV is such an addictive thing,
But I've one thing to say.
Whoever made it so,
If you watch you have to pay.

TV is such an irritating thing,
Installing the satellite panels.
So that you cannot watch,
Any of your nine hundred channels.

Harry Menear (11)
Rydon Community College

You Say

You say I am clever
But let me explain,
I live in a world
Where I appreciate knobbly knees.

Elliot Pretty (12)
Rydon Community College

The Traveller

(Inspired by 'The Listeners' by Walter de la Mare)

One dark eerie evening as night drew in
The traveller saddled up,
He headed to the manor house
No noise, not even a mouse,
As he got to the manor he felt a presence
He looked around but nobody was there,
He dismounted his horse and ran to the door
And with two gentle knocks he said, 'I was here, I swear,'
After he said those words he slung up his hood he was about
                                                    to mount his horse,
When it fled, fled into the settling moon
But the traveller did not see it coming from behind the door,
Nobody saw it coming
But now the traveller is no more.

William Underwood (11)
Rydon Community College

Autumn

The leaves are green
And also red.
Autumn is coming
Time for bed.

The leaves drop off the trees
It's time for insects to sleep.
Spring is round the corner
Waiting for the lambs to leap.

The sun drops below the hills
The sky deepens to red.
The air is cold and still
I think I'm ready for bed.

Alex Sturgess (11)
Rydon Community College

The Graveyard

As I creep silently forward
Into the cold dark night
The mist draws closer and closer
And the graveyard comes into sight.

I push open the rusty gate
Creaks shut behind me
Silent bats swoop in the moonlight
An owl hoots in the tree.

My heart is beating loudly
Pounding in my ears
I'm running faster and faster
Holding back the tears.

Shadows forming in the mist
My heart is pounding, running fast
Twigs snapping underfoot
Then, suddenly, home at last.

Jenny Finch (11)
Rydon Community College

The Moon

Gently, swiftly sun turns to moon,
Like a big silver balloon,
It's a silver ball being thrown into the atmosphere,
Now you can see that it's a sphere,
It's a sheet of ice moving gallantly across the sky
In their beds young children lie,
Water gleaming where the moon sets her rays,
Cattle in the field stop to graze,
She searches, she sees,
The birds in the trees.

Christopher Burton (11)
Rydon Community College

Narrative Poem

I leap out of bed
It's an exciting day,
I throw on my kit
I have a big match to play.

I arrive at the pitch
With the rest of my team,
We all did a warm-up
To play like a dream.

The ref blew his whistle
The match has begun,
Two goals before half-time
This game can be won.

Six goals follow
Their defence was a disaster,
A hat-trick by me
And I'm hailed as the master.

Daniel Andrews (11)
Rydon Community College

Fishing

I like fishing it makes me feel good,
I'd love to catch a big fish if I could.
Carp, trout, roach and pike,
I'm not fussy which one I like.

Sitting on a riverbank waiting for a fish,
My rod starts bending, *argh!* I wish.
Up through the water, pulling like mad,
Up comes the biggest fish I've ever had.

Karl Ray (11)
Rydon Community College

The Lady Of Shalott Part V

(Based On 'The Lady Of Shalott' by Alfred Lord Tennyson)

Her singing they could all still hear,
But down the river they stared with fear,
Bitter rain fell as she neared,
Children and women shedding a tear,
She floated down to Camelot.
And no longer shall she dream a place,
But as she whispered her last grace,
And feeling peace, she did praise
To die the Lady of Shalott.

No more breath in her was left,
Death of course the biggest theft,
Everything in her bereft,
No more life could have crept,
Into the Lady of Shalott.
The townsmen stared with wide eyes,
Women could not stop their cries,
People questioned with,'Why?'
In the town of Camelot.

Everyone did sob and weep,
For the lady who did sleep,
As unforgetful memories creep,
Not the ones you'd like to keep,
In the town of Camelot,
And so the story ends right here,
No happy endings, but many tears,
For the lady floating near,
The Lady of Shalott.

Amy-Jo Burt (12)
Rydon Community College

I Hate Writing Poetry

I hate writing poetry
Sitting in your room all day
Being bored and trying to think
When you could be going out to play.

I've tried eating apples
I've tried standing on my head
I've tried running round the garden
I've tried lying on my bed.

I just can't get any inspiration
Nothing comes to my mind
I used to like my English teacher
I used to think she was kind.

I don't want to think about poems
When I could be thinking about the school disco
Wearing all my fancy clothes
I'm going to dance with Steven Misko.

I've tried to speak to my father
I've tried to speak to my mother
My sister shouted, *'Go away'*
That just leaves my brother.

When I think of a poem
I'll write it down like poets do
Then give it to my teacher
For her to read to you.

Tasmine Graffy (11)
Rydon Community College

The Kestrel

Sharp eyes,
Sensitive ears,
Striking like a nightmare,
Gliding so softly,
Like ice cream
Trickling down your throat.

He glides so elegantly
Like a world famous romance novel
Striking like thunder
Shocking his prey
And no bird stands in his way.

The kestrel flies solo
No time for friends
His moves of flight
Are like an Olympic gymnast
In one of her sweet dreams.

A message from a kestrel
To a small bird
Please don't be afraid
Be terrified!

Harry Chalfont (10)
Rydon Community College

Leo The Lion!

There once was a lion called Leo,
Leo lived in the zoo,
He was desperate to escape,
But did not know how to.

The zoo was huge,
The zoo was mean,
The zoo was the loudest he had ever seen.

So one cold day,
Leo made a plan,
He needed to escape,
And get past the zookeeper man.

Leo found himself in the middle of a busy city,
It was dark,
It was cold,
There were lots of people young and old.

Leo decided he wanted to go home,
To his warm cosy place where he did not feel alone.

Sophie Wood (11)
Rydon Community College

The Lady Of Shalott, Part V

(Based On 'The Lady Of Shalott' by Alfred Lord Tennyson)

Her singing they could all still hear,
As she slowly floated near,
For the curse, they were full of fear,
Many people were drying a tear,
The people of Camelot.
The shiny, brave, glittery knight,
Showed his upset in villagers' sight,
As the flight of her spirit all in white,
The Lady of Shalott.

To catch her, Lancelot tried,
All the people surrounding cried,
He just wanted to be by her side,
He leapt into a freezing cold tide,
The knight, Sir Lancelot.
As he floated into shore,
The villagers cried some more,
At their heart strings it tore,
Dead with the Lady of Shalott.

Louise Wilson (13)
Rydon Community College

The Lady Of Shalott Part V

(Based On 'The Lady Of Shalott' by Alfred Lord Tennyson)

Her singing they could all still hear,
They didn't know her spirit was near,
When it arose, they were filled with fear,
Its high-pitched singing, they could hear,
All over Camelot.
Then, behind them, passed the hearse,
Lancelot wished he could reverse,
The horrible, dreadful, killing curse,
And help the Lady of Shalott.

As she passed, the ladies cried,
Because the Lady had sadly died,
Sir Lancelot sighed and sighed,
His face, he was desperately trying to hide,
Away from Camelot.
The sky turned from blue to grey,
It was a horrible, dreary, mourning day,
The people had begun to pray,
For the Lady of Shalott.

Stacey Ranger (13)
Rydon Community College